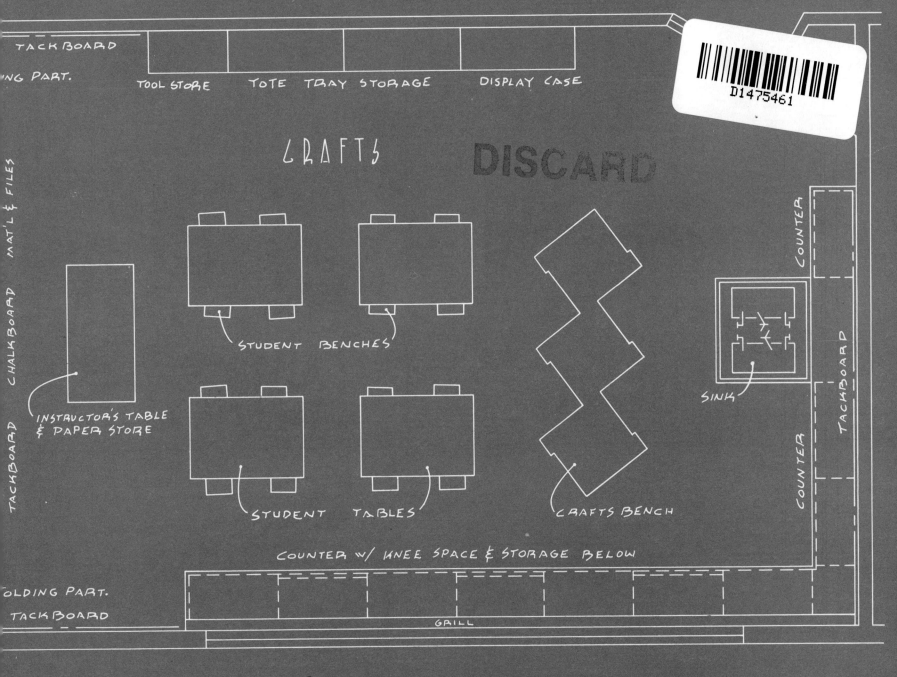

TACKBOARD

NG PART.

TOOL STORE   TOTE TRAY STORAGE   DISPLAY CASE

CRAFTS

DISCARD

MAT'L & FILES

CHALKBOARD

TACKBOARD

COUNTER

COUNTER

TACKBOARD

STUDENT BENCHES

SINK

INSTRUCTOR'S TABLE
& PAPER STORE

STUDENT TABLES

CRAFTS BENCH

COUNTER w/ KNEE SPACE & STORAGE BELOW

OLDING PART.

TACKBOARD

GRILL

RTMENT

A QUALITATIVE PROGRAM FOR THE YOUNG ADOLESCENT

ART IN DEPTH

A QUALITATIVE PROGRAM FOR THE YOUNG ADOLESCENT

ART IN DEPTH

FRANK WACHOWIAK
Professor of Art
The University of Georgia

DAVID HODGE
Assistant Professor of Art
State University of Wisconsin

INTERNATIONAL TEXTBOOK COMPANY
An Intext Publisher
Scranton, Pennsylvania 18515

AN INTERNATIONAL TEXTBOOK IN ART AND ART EDUCATION

Color reproduction for title page courtesy of American Telephone and Telegraph Company. Book design and color photography by the authors. Supplemental black and white photography by W. Robert Nix.

To Mary and Lamar Dodd

PREFACE

Because the teachers of art in schools, colleges, and universities responded so enthusiastically to the recently published *Emphasis: Art,* International Textbook Company, Scranton, Pennsylvania, 1965, which describes high-caliber art practices in the elementary school program, it occurred to us that a similarly designed text emphasizing qualitative art goals, projects, and programming for the junior high or middle school might be as warmly welcomed.

Prompted by the good wishes of our colleagues and motivated by the contagious enthusiasm of former students whose dedicated teaching has enriched the lives of the young adolescents they instruct, as well as our own, we have documented verbally and visually those strategies, methods, evaluations, and objectives which we believe can provide continuity, scope, and purpose for secondary school art programs, especially those involving the critical junior high area.

Observations of art classes in action in a number of countries around the world have convinced us that there is no substitute for the enthusiastic, informed, confident, and prepared teacher. Consequently we have tried to present as realistically and unequivocally as possible specific guidelines that can help teachers of today and tomorrow plan and implement junior high school art programs of promise and achievement.

This book, like *Emphasis: Art,* is the result of many years of actual involvement with youngsters in art classes. It describes factual situations, not theoretical ones. Except where noted otherwise, the reproductions of art in this text represent the creative efforts of young adolescents from middle schools or junior high schools both here and abroad. The colorful, exciting illustrations prove that the challenge and adventure of creating fine art does not end with the child; that young adolescents, too, can be equally expressive and evocative in their visual responses if only their teachers are wise enough, patient enough, and willing enough to guide them.

Despite our concern to deal specifically with those teaching strategies germane to the early teenage years, the discriminating reader may discover that the basic premises and convictions implicit in *Emphasis: Art* are recapitulated and reaffirmed in several instances in this book. It is our hope that this art guide can be used by college art education faculties and by art consultants in the field as a companion text to *Emphasis: Art,* so that students preparing to be teachers and teachers now in service can benefit from seeing how a planned sequence of in-depth art learnings from grade one through nine contributes to significant, qualitative performance and achievement.

For their kind assistance in helping us research the visual material for this book, we are indebted to Professor Alan Turner, Manchester, England; David H. Tyler of the *London Sunday Mirror;* Wolfram Quante of the Pelikan Company, Hannover, West Germany; Sukumar Shankar Pillai, Editor *Shankar's Weekly,* New Delhi, India and in Japan to Professor Keiichi Mori of Chiba University; Professor Mineo Kozuma of Osaka Liberal Arts University; Tadaaki Akashi and Yoshiro Aoki of Sakura Color Products Corporation; Eiichi Moriyama of Japan Stationery Company Ltd.; Professor Mutsuya Fujita of Kyoto; Professor Isshi Kamishima and Masanori Suzuki of Nara; Saburo Kurata and Ota Koshi, Editor of *Hanga,* Tokyo.

Our gratitude goes to the many junior high and middle school art teachers in England, West Germany, Italy, Greece, India, Hongkong, Japan, and the United States who extended cordial invitations to observe their classes in action and who provided us with selections of their students' creative work. We appreciate the efforts of Dr. W. Robert Nix of the University of Georgia Art Department who processed many of the black and white illustrations and permitted the use of the original nature studies from his unpublished 1968 doctoral dissertation, "Nature's Precedents for Design—A Photographic Analysis."

Our highest accolades, of course, go to those youngsters whose creative efforts have made this book a visual delight—the young adolescents, here and abroad, whose sense of wonder and joy in discovery continually renew our own commitment to teaching.

FRANK WACHOWIAK
DAVID HODGE

Athens, Georgia
December 1969

CONTENTS

1

INTRODUCTION

In a day and age when we are confronted with a plethora of non-art manifestations, when schools of "minimal," "funk" and "soul" expression are the rule rather than the exception, and when art is sometimes defined as *anything one can get by with,* the appearance of a teacher's guidebook dealing with the qualitative, the serious, the planned and the purposeful in art may seem somewhat reactionary or anachronistic. Yet now, more than ever before, it is vitally important that we reemphasize the acquisition and implementation of art fundamentals as a worthy goal for our students and for ourselves. The youngsters in our classes are entitled to the most, not the least, we can give them. This means a renewal of our commitment to teach the substance, the content, and the structure of art. It is our business, our responsibility.

There may be eye-popping and shocking developments taking place in the avant-garde ateliers of New York, London and San Francisco, but the typical middle or junior high school art teacher must still meet the crowded Monday through Friday classes, must still plan something worthwhile to keep the youngsters interested and busy five or more hours each day, and must still perform those hundred-and-one routine teaching tasks that have little in common with the way-out, bizarre and self-indulgent "happenings" that many of today's art editors praise so vociferously and indiscriminately. Their unrestricted kudos for the "novel" and the "entertaining" leads one to suspect a minor conspiracy afoot to pressure an unaware public into acknowledging the gimmicky and the mediocre as acceptable and standard art performance.

Teachers who plan the art programs in our schools must be realistic. They cannot afford to take their cues from the majority of contemporary art shows currently on view in the metropolitan galleries. The in-vogue styles change with every season, and no art teacher, much less his students, can keep up with them. What teachers need to emphasize in their school programs are those perennial art values, premises and aesthetic concerns that function for today as well as for tomorrow. With strong art convictions to guide

Opposite Page—Adolescents everywhere find deep satisfaction and challenge in on-the-scene drawing and painting. The teacher should provide ample opportunities for sketching field trips as a vital part of the art program.

1

them, they will find they can challenge young adolescents to move beyond normal expectancies and create individual, exciting interpretations of real worth.

A major part of this book concerns itself with the *creation of art*. This emphasis is purposeful. The teaching of art in our schools is still weakest and most unimaginative at that critical point where the teacher attempts to discuss and evaluate the student's work-in-process. The most successful teaching, the most worthwhile evaluative strategies, are based on understanding art structure and implementing the vocabulary and language of art as a key factor in learning. Art fundamentals must be identified, reinforced and repeated at every stage of the program, in every project, until they become a working, vital part of the youngster's expressive repertoire.

The teaching approach described in this text is recommended for students in grades six through nine of middle schools or junior high schools. In some communities the seventh and possibly the eighth grade classes are part of the elementary school system, but the problems of teaching art to the young adolescent during these critical years are typically alike whether he has moved to a separate junior-high complex or still attends classes in an elementary schoolroom.

Unlike senior high school classes in studio art which are elective, meet daily, and are comparatively small in size, seventh and eighth grade art in most schools is usually a required subject, the classes are large (sometimes as many as 35 students per class), and the time

2

Top—Students on a field trip to a local nursery find inspiration for drawing in the many varieties of plant forms. Center—A classmate becomes the most immediate subject for in-depth sketching. Bottom—Student using magazine ad colors as his painting medium. Note his space-filling preliminary drawing.

allotted is often a small fraction of that scheduled for the *solid* subjects. Young adolescents who are required to take art demand an entirely different tactical approach on the part of the teacher than advanced adolescents who elect art courses. Crowded seventh and eighth grade art classes present more complex organizational problems than the smaller senior high elective classes. The early adolescent of twelve to fifteen years of age requires a much more sympathetic and sensitive understanding on the part of the teacher than does the more mature senior high school student.

One of the most effective approaches to understanding and appreciating the arts is through actual involvement in the creative act itself. Adolescents who become aware of the possibilities and potential of the art aesthetic, of line, shape, value, color, pattern, texture, space, form, emphasis, rhythm, tension, and symmetry in their own work develop a greater sensitivity to the formal and design aspects in the arts they encounter. For example, youngsters who have seriously and successfully engaged in a multi-media collage undertaking where the significant demands and characteristic quality of the technique have been emphasized and assimilated, respond more readily and critically to the collages of George Braque, Pablo Picasso, Kurt Schwitters, Alberto Burri, Conrad Marca-Relli and contemporary collagists.

There is a need, especially at the secondary school level, for sound strategies in the critical appraisal of works of art, but nothing can substitute for the student's actual involvement in qualitative art experiences with the corollary motivational references to artists and their art, past and present, as a basis for meaningful appreciation of the arts.

Left—During a "found" materials collage project, the working areas become cluttered. Sufficient time must be allowed for clean-up so that materials can be stored properly. Right— These youngsters made preliminary sketches, gathered "found" materials in neutral colors, then using their compositions as a guide, completed these collages on heavy cardboard or masonite.

2
THE YOUNG ADOLESCENT

The junior high school youngster moves into a changed academic world in which for the first time he may have a different teacher for each subject he takes. Unless he has left the elementary school with a growing assurance that art is a rewarding, challenging and worthwhile experience in which he can successfully participate, the secondary school teacher faces a most difficult task of developing in the adolescent an enthusiastic and genuine response to art. If he has come from the typical elementary situation where the classroom teacher taught art, it will be his first contact with a special art teacher. It is important that this initial contact be a sympathetic yet stimulating one. He should recognize in his art teacher the same confidence, the same conviction, the same enthusiasm that he sees in the best science or mathematics teacher.

Too often the junior high art instructor thinks of the early adolescent as a child with childish interests and abilities. The teacher should not expect wonders of the young teenager, but neither should he underrate his potential and unique capabilities. The maturing youngster now can thrive on complex and difficult tasks, but he will need to be guided and encouraged to develop perceptive and creative skills augmented by a growing vocabulary and language of art.

The junior high adolescent is experiencing a renaissance of awareness and self-consciousness, of sensitivity to differences in others, of identification with others, of rediscovery and appreciation of his world, of heightened emotional response, and of intellectual inquisitiveness which in some cases may never be matched again. In many ways he is less inhibited than the upper elementary school child, but he is still highly critical of his own performance. He is more willing to tackle new processes, new materials, and new ideas. He is technically more proficient, his ability to capitalize on suggestions is sharpened, and he can now enter more intelligently into critical discussions on art form, structure and content. His cultural horizons are increasingly expanding, and it is vitally important at this stage to acquaint him with the best of the fine arts, crafts and architecture. He is at the moment highly impressionable and may carry the sensitivities, preferences and prejudices he develops in the junior high

Opposite Page—Terra cotta clay structure, life size, by a young adolescent. England. Courtesy of LONDON SUNDAY MIRROR.

years with him the rest of his life.

It is in these *middle schools* or junior high schools that the teacher really begins to see the personalities of students reflected in their art. There he discovers the introvert, the extrovert, the timid, the reckless, the methodical, the haphazard, the moody, the scientific, the plodder, the maverick, the perfectionist, the dreamer, the braggadocio, the loner, and the idealist.

Teachers should remember that the young adolescent is very vulnerable emotionally. Direct criticism of his work in front of his classmates can be humiliating for him. Sarcasm and belittling remarks should be avoided at all costs. Do not embarrass him, either, by praising his efforts too overtly or indiscriminately in the presence of his peers.

Adolescents are sometimes apathetic or cool in their response to art, to drawing, painting and printmaking, but once they are caught up in the exciting technical possibilities and results, they are avid converts to the cause. It is the teacher's responsibility to help make the art world come alive for them, to involve them so fully in the act of art that they are *committed almost unaware*. When this fortuitous development takes place, they almost resent the termination of the art period, the disturbances caused by their classmates, even the intrusion of the teacher's voice itself.

For more data on the young adolescent's characteristics and clues to his behavior, the reader is referred to Appendix A.

The young adolescent today is intrigued by the new psychedelic colors and shapes. Here students created self-portraits or portraits of their classmates to fit a circle shape. They made preliminary drawings in white chalk on assorted color construction paper and then completed the painting in oil pastel. (See page 91.)

Group mural project began with actual sketches of students playing instruments. Oil pastel on 24" X 36" colored construction paper. Exploitation of unusual pattern and color was emphasized (grade 7). University Schools, Oshkosh, Wisconsin.

Illustrations in this chapter are works of students in the art
education classes, University of Georgia, Athens. Here future
teachers of art sketch from colorfully attired models. One
result, a tempera-India ink batik showing the process before
and after the inking and rinsing.

3
THE TEACHER'S ROLE

There is perhaps no keener challenge that novice art teachers must face than the teaching of adolescents at the junior high school level. At the same time, there is no greater satisfaction than that of discovering and encouraging the unique art potential of these youngsters caught between childhood and adulthood. It is particularly important that art in this transitional period be taught as skillfully, dramatically and purposefully as possible because it is in these critical years that students decide for or against advanced courses in art and often for art as a career. A more vital reason for qualitative and dynamic teaching is that junior high school art courses are terminal for most students, and the impressions gained concerning art and art values during this period are apt to be lasting ones.

If a student becomes bored or learns to dislike art in the junior high school, it is unlikely that he will elect it in senior high school or college. If he is allowed to flounder and fail in art performance because the teacher is not qualified to guide and inspire him, he develops a negative attitude toward the art class and often toward art as a whole. The young adolescent needs a highly dedicated and prepared teacher to bring out the best in him, to expand his vision, and to stretch his world to the farthest boundaries.

Wherever art programs of exciting and qualitative dimensions exist, whether in the junior high or middle schools of England, Germany, India, Japan or the United States, one always discovers in the wings an enthusiastic, personable and gifted teacher who is deeply involved in his own creative growth, in his teaching responsibilities, in the youngsters he instructs, and in the wonders of life itself. The best teacher, whether in the smallest school or the smallest town, begins with his very first teaching assignment to implement and build a vital art awareness in his students, his school and his community. He believes wholeheartedly in the unique rejuvenating effects of the art experience. He has strong convictions concerning the qualitative in art, and he continues to grow as a creative person. Eschewing the ordinary, he distills and emphasizes those practices in art consistent with the needs of his students, keenly aware that the most vital art is identified and concerned with the difficult, the time-consuming and the passionate, not with the cursory, superficial or lukewarm.

The teacher's effectiveness in the art class is heightened considerably if he has had opportunities to explore and create successfully with the same tools and materials available to his students. It is important that the teacher discover the unique, aesthetic possibilities of ordinary crayon, clay, watercolors, tempera, colored construction paper, linoleum for printmaking, oil pastels and other inexpensive art media or "found" objects.

High-caliber college or university art methods courses should provide studio experiences for this type of qualitative exploration and discovery. The teacher then can implement these learnings in the everyday situations he will find in his own classes with his students.

The reaffirmation of the guiding role of the art teacher in the junior high school is more critical today than ever before. There are influences at work, unfortunately some in the education profession itself, that are undermining the teacher's importance and responsibility.

The art instructor must feel he is more than custodian or dispenser of tools and materials if he hopes to maintain his effectiveness and self-respect as a teacher. He must sense that his guidance and expertise in art are genuinely needed by his students. At the same time he must possess a strong conviction in the worth of the art program he plans.

One of six panels created by graduate art education majors, University of Georgia, for display at the Southeast Regional Art Education Conference, Atlanta, emphasizing the importance of visuals in teaching and the implementation of art techniques gained in college.

Three 12″ × 18″ examples of the crayon engraving technique with supplementary oil pastel areas. College students discover, often to their own surprise, they can use commonly available school art materials to produce fine art of significant aesthetic worth. They can then implement these learnings in their own teaching.

11

Wherever adolescent art programs of merit exist, they do so mainly because of the organized, knowledgeable and creative efforts of an artist-teacher. One can immediately sense the electric involvement, the purposefulness of effort, the genuine rapport between student and teacher when one visits an art room *where the art experience is considered important and where qualitative art learning is taking place.*

Creative teaching demands imagination, empathy, insight, patience and courage, especially the courage to disavow the trite, to attempt new techniques, to make decisions involving student progress in art.

The art teacher is continually faced with the problem of what project to select, when to present it, and how much time to devote to it. The teacher of the adolescent assumes nothing. Unlike teachers in mathematics, science and social studies who build on sequential elementary school learnings, the junior high art teacher must often plan on introducing the students to a basic art vocabulary and to fundamental art concepts before he can begin to implement a quality program.

High-caliber art teaching, like any other successful venture, is a synthesis of many individual tasks done exceedingly well.

The everyday wax crayon on colored paper has rich, exciting possibilities as these 12″ × 18″ "still-life" studies attest. Teachers who discover the crayon's potential can help youngsters in art more effectively. Encourage discovery of new color combinations through color over color.

The best junior high school art instructors do the following to make their teaching day, their classroom and their school a living lesson in art:

Plan the year's or semester's art program in advance,
Organize field trips and visits to galleries and museums,
Explore exciting new sites for sketching possibilities,
Search for and acquire interesting objects to use as visual stimulation,
Arrange displays of student work in hallways, cafeteria, principal's office and civic centers,
Plan and expedite needed storage and display facilities,
Record resource visuals and student's projects in color slides and black and white photography,
Acquire a library of color slides, reproductions, publications, and filmstrips,
Experiment with and test new art materials,
Keep in touch with the latest developments in art education,
Arrange exhibits from other schools, other countries,
Invite guest artists to talk to their students,
Order and screen films for their classes,
Write evaluative comments on students' work-in-progress,
Prepare stimulating presentations on art appreciation,
Meet with students after school on special projects,
Organize materials for technique demonstrations,
Make the art room a unique and stimulating environment.

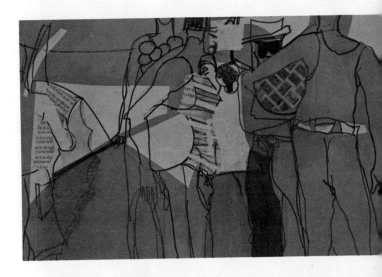

The collage with "found" materials has countless possibilities. Here a preliminary sketch from actual student models becomes the starting point of an exciting colorful 18″ × 24″ collage. Note successful handling of space, overlapping, varying heights of figures, and lines leading into composition.

13

The prepared, enthusiastic, and confident instructor of art who responds to youngsters, who builds on the adolescents' previous art learnings, who provides them with new aesthetic and perceptual challenges, and who enriches their lives by initiating and developing unique motivational material for his classes earns the admiration and respect of his students, and ensures his own identifiable role and purpose as a teacher.

14

Affinity of materials was stressed in these "found" material collages which began with a preliminary sketch on the scene, except in the assemblage at the lower left. Emphasis was called to effective utilization of neutral, subtle colors and texture. Repetition of a color, shape, value, or pattern was a factor in achieving unity.

A remarkable print made by engraving into a glossy-coated cardboard with pin, needle, compass point, or X-acto knife, then inking with felt dauber using printing oil ink, wiping off glossy areas with paper towels, and then printing on slightly moist white drawing or construction paper. A heavy-duty roller press must be used.

Opposite Page, Top Left—Multi-crayon engraving. Middle and Bottom Left—Process before and after engraving. Right—Tempera-India ink batik. Middle and Bottom Right —Process before inking and rinsing. This Page, Left—A linoleum print inspired by a photograph in LIFE. Right—The linoleum block is printed over a magazine color page.

4
AVENUES TO MOTIVATION

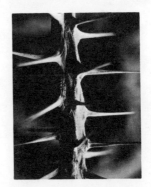

A continuing concern of the successful art teacher are those strategies of stimulation, motivation, provocation and pump-priming that can be implemented effectively to make the art program richer and more purposeful for his students. Instructors agree that before personal, meaningful and vital art expression takes place, the youngster must have rich experiences that can trigger his visual interpretation, and he must develop those perceptive and creative skills that can give his effort artistic life.

The teacher can turn on occasion to the current activities of the young adolescent to suggest possible subject matter for their projects. Teenagers who respond enthusiastically to the new singing groups, to sports heroes and to the astronauts' achievements in space, can easily be encouraged to use their interests as a starting point for paintings, prints and sculpture.

The most effective motivations, teachers find, are usually at their own doorsteps. Art instructors have learned to guide their students to see the possibilities for subject content in the trees, flowers and shrubbery in the immediate environment; in the aquariums, plants and mounted specimens in the school's science department; in the musical instruments of the school's orchestra or band; in assorted sports equipment from the athletic department; in the cafeteria at lunchtime, the view from a window or down a hallway, activities in the school gym, students waiting for the school bus, and in the homecoming festivities. It is always advisable to obtain permission to sketch in certain areas to prevent interference with classes in session or personnel on duty. The teacher should check school regulations in all cases.

Sometimes teachers may find their schools are located in a motivational wasteland, such as a school built on a prairie with not a tree or house in sight, an art room without a window for viewing, a metropolitan structure sandwiched between cement and brick. In these situations the teacher must turn to those motivational resources he can actually bring to the students and to the class. Among these are the "found" objects for a still-life arrangement; the costumes and assorted paraphernalia students can utilize for figure-drawing projects; the pets, gold fish, dogs,

cats or birds commandeered to be models; the bicycles, motorcycles and guitars that can be rounded up.

The big city youngster, surrounded by sky-high building complexes, traffic jams and incessant urban noise will often express his reactions and impressions in subject matter that is more complex in content than that of the rural or small town adolescent whose world is one of open farms and quiet neighborhoods. However, movies, radio, records and the ubiquitous TV set are closing the gap so that youngsters as far apart as New York, Seattle or Albuquerque now may respond to similar motivations.

Skilled art teachers do not introduce art projects in the same way each time, nor do they fall into a set routine for meeting their class once the project is underway. They know that the youngster engaged in art needs more than a perfunctory "OK, let's get busy!" to stir him to greater performance. They utilize every possible resource at their disposal to make the art experience an important one in the lives of their students. Music, television, pantomime, poetry, films, color slides, dance, photography, drama, current magazines and news stories are all part of their art teaching repertoire. They realize, too, that the final stages of a project are very often just as crucial to its qualitative success as the preliminary efforts. It is during the critical later stages that a certain ennui or operational fatigue may develop which the teacher must be prepared to counteract with additional motivational ammunition. In expressive techniques such as crayon, crayon engraving, collage and plaster reliefs, it is often

Youngsters can often find inspiration for paintings in their immediate neighborhood, whether they come from a farm, a small town, or a large city. Top—Manchester, England. Center— Riverside, Iowa. Bottom—Osaka, Japan.

Subject ideas for art projects can often be found in the student's immediate environment abounding with plants, shells, or rocks. Macrophotography. Courtesy of Dr. W. Robert Nix, University of Georgia.

the final resolutions and refinements that give the work its vitality and individual quality. Conversely, a project can be easily jeopardized by over-working detail and texture. The teacher and student must learn to recognize when restraint is called for.

One of the art teacher's greatest challenges is to turn adolescents into noticers, avid noticers of their environment. The girl or boy who notices the shape of panes in windows, the unique cornice of a door, the intricate latch on a cabinet, the subtle patina on a sculpture, the moving reflections in water, the varied cracks in dry mudbanks, the shadow of a tree against a house or the veins in a leaf, is the youngster who brings deeper insights and expanding visual resources to his art expression and lives a richer, more rewarding life. If the teacher can bring the student to really look at the uniqueness of things, he will make him an inquisitive explorer all his life.

The concerned and growing art teacher utilizes every possible avenue to open the eyes of his students to the world he lives in. Photography and film making, which offer the challenge and excitement of a relatively new media, can be introduced at the junior high school level to heighten the youngster's perceptual and visual awareness. Students can be encouraged to make photographic and film documentation of a variety of subject matter that can be effectively used as motivation for their art. Photography and film making, if taught creatively, will sensitize the student's selective, seeing eye. Art expression inspired by the photographic or filmed image will call upon their inner vision as well. For the teacher of adolescents, a college or university course in basic photography or film making is essential today.

5

TEACHING STRATEGIES

The junior high school art teacher is commonly "blessed" with a full day's responsibilities. In most cases one class follows another without pause, making the art room a beehive of activity. It is the fortunate teacher, indeed, who has a free class period to prepare materials and plan succeeding art lessons. Because of his multiple responsibilities, it is singularly important that the teacher plan his teaching strategy a week, a month, a semester, or even a year in advance.

The first week of school, especially the first class meetings, are crucial in the building of a qualitative program. It is a wise teacher who prepares adequately for these initial sessions with his students, and if he chooses to emulate other successful programs, he might begin the campaign with the art room itself.

The art room's appearance reflects the teacher's art convictions and his awareness of design as a vital environmental factor. *The art room's impact on the students on the opening day of school is, in fact, the teacher's first lesson.* The room should be inviting and visually stimulating, not a cold, clinical laboratory. The experienced teacher relies on a variety of resources, including "found" objects, attractive bulletin displays, plants and natural forms, art reproductions, giant posters, mobiles, mounted birds and animals, artifacts, butterfly, insect or shell collections, original works of art, an aquarium, art book displays, examples of student art work, and selected antiques or Americana, *to make the art room a perpetually changing world of wonders.*

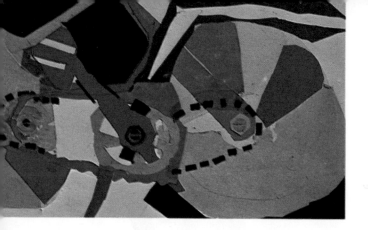

It is important to begin the studio experiences with a project which the teacher is qualified to handle and in which all students can achieve some measure of success. Highly recommended for an initial project is a colored construction paper *collage* which provides many opportunities for introducing and emphasizing design and compositional factors of shape, positive and negative space, variety, overlapping forms, value, pattern and color. Refer to the section on Collage in Chapter 8 for a more detailed coverage of this project. Some other suggested introductory art activities are: "found" object printing on tissue collage or on colored construction paper with oil pastel variations, tempera paint explorations on colored paper, or *frottage* i.e. rubbed designs utilizing natural source textures as inspirational material.

Because junior high school students come from diverse backgrounds, possessing varying elementary school preparations, the teacher will welcome any information that will make his role more effective, more purposeful, and more sympathetic. Assignment of a brief written autobiography on the first day of class may elicit some pertinent responses including the nature of art experiences the youngsters had in grade school, projects they enjoyed the most, famous artists they have read about, hobbies, special interests, part-time jobs, careers they are planning, galleries and museums they have visited, and travel to foreign countries.

For a majority of students entering junior high school, the studio art room with its special furniture, strange equipment and tools will be a new world, a

Top—Collage of colored construction paper inspired by the structure of a bicycle. Center—Potato print on colored construction paper with additional background shapes in oil pastel. Bottom—Collage limited to the black, white and printed areas from magazines. Background is colored construction paper.

new experience. It is a sound move, therefore, to brief the students on the first day of class concerning the use of the room and its facilities. Experienced teachers find that a list of regulations dealing with proper maintenance of the room, equipment and tools is very helpful. A copy of these regulations may be given to each student and a larger printed form posted in the art room. Included in this list should be clear instructions for proper use and care of work areas, kilns, printing presses, silk-screen frames, looms, drawing boards, brushes, scissors, paper cutters, brayers, drills, metal rasps, cutting and carving tools, storage areas, ceramic and banding wheels, staplers, wedging boards and soldering irons or torches. Certain supply cupboards or closets may be designated "off limits" to all students except monitors.

Veteran art teachers know there is no single solution to the varied behavioral problems they must cope with. Every beginning teacher must resolve disciplinary issues in his own way, but experienced art instructors have found it is much wiser to begin classes with a serious, organized approach which can be modified later if the situation warrants it, than to allow so much freedom that it is impossible to bring the class under control when necessary. If the students suspect that the teacher is unconcerned when they waste time in idle chatter, they will develop a laissez faire attitude in art class. It is a proven fact, moreover, that the quality of art expression or performance diminishes as the ratio of loud talking and socializing increases. The teacher may find it expedient to suggest

a code of behavior for the art room similar to the regulations set up for proper use of facilities. Students should ordinarily remain in assigned seats during class unless given permission by the teacher to move about. In large classes students should take turns obtaining and returning materials and tools, either by tables or rows. Excessive talking, whistling, running, shouting, throwing things at one another, immoderate personal grooming, propping feet on desks, table-hopping, crowding at sink areas, leaning out of windows and gum chewing should be discouraged as much as possible.

The practice of the teacher meeting the students at the door at the beginning of the period is recommended. A cheerful greeting by the teacher can start the class off in the right mood. If there is a tendency on the part of some incoming students to be boisterous and distracting, this problem can be resolved at its origin. Sometimes a brief directive can be made as students enter regarding the procedure for the period. Students then can proceed to work without wasted time. This strategy is doubly important in schools where minutes are doled out to the art program.

The machinery of distributing student work-in-process, art supplies and tools should be thought out carefully by the teacher *before the class begins*. Much valuable time is often wasted because the instructor did not plan this phase of the art lesson. The return of student work-in-process can be expedited by making sure that youngsters put their names on their works. Class monitors can check this. Paper should be cut to required sizes before the class meets. A wasteful bottleneck is created by students awaiting their turn at the paper cutter. Materials can be distributed quickly through a student monitor system or by having students come up by rows or tables to a central supply area.

The teacher should check and make sure beforehand that there will be an adequate supply of art materials for the whole class, enough paper, paint, brushes, pencils, scissors, paste and other items that the project requires. Class management and disciplinary problems often arise when supplies run short and students without needed materials have extra time on their hands.

Getting the class off to a good start is a major step in the establishment of a productive atmosphere. The experienced teacher generally waits until he has the attention of all the students before he presents the assignments or gives demonstrations. In some instances he may have to remind the class to settle down. When possible, he should make sure students understand the project's goals and objectives, repeating directions when necessary. However, he should not stretch out the motivational, demonstration or critique sessions longer than called for and must be on the alert for unmistakable signs of disinterest: the shuffle of chairs, the tapping and dropping of pencils, the whispering conspiracies, and the far-away, dreamy look. There is a fatigue point in teenage response, and the teacher must gauge his hold on the students. Adolescents want information and elucidation, it is true, but they also want to get at their work. A perceptive teacher can detect when students are half-listening, more intent on some distracting gadget in their possession than on the teacher's remarks. When an expert teacher spots a wandering prodigal, he brings him back with a question, a reprimand or quite simply with a pause and a look in the offender's direction. One word of advice about class control bears repeating. When a teacher plans to have a discussion prior to studio activity, it is recommended that materials and tools not be distributed until after the discussion period because too many students are naturally tempted to explore the materials in question instead of giving full attention to the teacher's presentation.

Clean-up procedures should be as orderly as possible. It is wiser to allot sufficient time for clean-up than to wait until the last moment and create conditions which generate confusion. The time needed for efficient clean-up will vary with different projects and should be allotted accordingly.

The wise teacher dismisses the class in an orderly fashion as soon as monitors and students have completed routine housekeeping tasks and have returned to their assigned seats. Discourage the practice of permitting students who finish their clean-up early to position themselves at the door like track sprinters at take-off. If some moments remain after clean-up, the teacher should use this time in a positive way, rather than let the period terminate in conversational chaos and purposelessness. Occasionally a summing-up, an evaluative or recapitulative session at the close of the period is recommended, but sufficient time must be budgeted for such a practice.

The common complaint of students is that teachers have eyes in the back of their head and are aware of every student trick or misdemeanor. This, of course, is an overstatement, but it is important that the teacher know what is going on in the classroom and be at strategic places at strategic times. During material distribution it is recommended that the teacher be in the vicinity of the supply area to expedite matters. When lecturing, the teacher should avoid standing in front of windows since this forces the students to face the glare of light. In the best situations the instructor moves among the students during the studio period, making suggestions when necessary, rather than stationing himself at his desk. Too much time is wasted when students have to wait in a queue. The experienced teacher does not let himself get side-tracked or beleaguered by the demands of a bevy of questioning students at a time when he should be monitoring the class as a whole, especially during the opening minutes of class and at clean-up time. If necessary, he should make it known that he will advise only one student at a time, reminding the youngsters to take turns when conferring with him.

The blackboard and bulletin board can be the teacher's most effective aids in presenting project procedures and in helping students evaluate their own efforts without relying on personal confrontations with the teacher. The best teachers do not rely on verbal instructions alone. They complement them with the written word, with visual displays, with process charts

DON QUIXOTE by *college art education major. An 8″ × 14″ plaster relief from a clay negative mold. Note how the oval shape encloses the figure and adds to the mood of dejection.*

of a technique and with specific evaluative questions on the blackboard that the students can refer to while they are engaged in their projects. Naturally, all these written aids are reinforced by the teacher's personal involvement with each student.

Problems of student rebellion, apathy, and disinterest in art class are almost always the result of insufficient planning, vague or misunderstood objectives, unrealistic goals or outcomes, meager motivations, a paucity of visual resources and stimulation, insufficient technical know-how, weak rapport between teacher and student, or a lack of conviction about the worth of the art experience.

For the novice art teacher the first semester or first year of teaching can be critical in many respects. To keep his enthusiasm and dedication high, the new teacher must sense a certain confidence and pride in the job he is doing. Being prepared for each lesson, each class meeting, each student challenge, helps the teacher develop that confidence. The prepared art teacher plans the discussion, demonstration or evaluation sessions well in advance. He does not count on last-minute inspirations. Generally he outlines his strategy in a planning notebook or similar device, knowing that in the excitement a discussion engenders, he may forget to emphasize important aspects of the project. Because the time allotted to art in many schools is minimal, the teacher must phrase his questioning to bring out the richest responses in the shortest time. The teacher must learn, too, to utilize every possible audio and visual means at his command to clarify technical processes and expedite evaluation of the student work-in-progress. Teachers of other subjects often infer that the art teacher is fortunate because he does not have papers to correct and other related homework. They forget that art teachers spend many hours planning projects, organizing supplies and tools, putting up student displays, and serving as supervisors of stage scenery or yearbooks. The best art teachers also take time after school or evenings to review student work-in-process and make notations accompanying the work that will help the student re-evaluate his efforts and improve his performance.

Getting to know the students is especially important in student-teacher rapport. The instructor should make a seating chart and learn the names of the students as early as possible. Make the chart with moveable tabs so changes in seating arrangements can be made if necessary.

Before studio activity begins, inform the students where specifically needed materials and tools are stored and where work-in-progress is to be stored, reminding them that the successful functioning of an art class depends upon the cooperation of everyone in class.

In carrying out a project, stress only one or two objectives each class period. Do not confuse the students with too many directives or suggestions at once. In a drawing project, for example, during the first session try emphasizing the *effective utilization of space*. On the second day, the students might be guided to evaluate the *variety* of shapes and overlapping planes in their drawing and to make constructive changes. During the third class meeting, the teacher might challenge the youngsters to enrich their drawings through *texture, pattern* and *value* contrasts.

As often as possible, take time to discuss the students' efforts with them. They need to grow in the ability to evaluate themselves and their work from many points of view. Teachers will learn that this kind of dialogue between student and mentor, though not always easy to achieve, is in the long run the most rewarding.

Adolescents perform at different rates of speed; therefore the teacher must plan additional assignments for those who complete their projects first. Girls are usually more deliberate and neater in their tasks than boys at this age and may need more time to complete their work. The teacher will find that he has to devote more of his time and energy to challenging the boys in class to set higher standards of performance for themselves.

Try all possible avenues of motivation, of reasoning and of strategic reconciliation before resorting to chastisement of any sort, whether it be sending the student out into the hall, moving him to another table, or referring him to the principal.

As a rule, do not act hastily in the matter of disciplining a student. Do not mete out punishment during the heat of the crisis. Admonish the student and tell him you will discuss the infraction after class or after school. Be fair in your dealing with all the students. Students sense and resent a teacher who plays favorites.

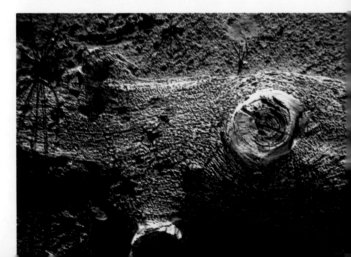

One of the art teacher's major roles is to encourage the students to be noticers—avid noticers of their constantly changing environment. It is vital that they became aware of the myriads of colors, forms, patterns, and textures in the world of nature.

31

Once the teacher has stipulated a punishment for a student or students, he should carry it out. Students learn to take advantage of the instructor who continually threatens or promises punitive measures but never acts on them.

Teachers of junior high school students must realize beforehand that the young adolescent has a need to communicate and that talking in class can be a common occurrence, especially during studio activity. However, when the talking or noise decibel becomes so disturbing that it prevents concentration on the project-in-process, the teacher must take action. How he does this may be critical. If he shouts "Quiet!" or "Settle down!", raps a desk with a ruler, rings a bell, or claps his hands, he may be successful in calming the class for a while. Veteran teachers use a more positive, more constructive approach. Calling the class to attention, they emphasize some aspect of the project that needs amplification or clarification or, displaying some of the students' work-in-progress, they point out specifically creative solutions. In this strategy the teacher achieves the objective of restoring order without resorting to repetitive epithet or abuse, and so avoids becoming a martinet in the eyes of his students.

There is no doubt whatsoever that the class that has been highly motivated, that has been guided to see the many possibilities of the technique or project, will be less likely to cause disturbance. It has been documented, moreover, that in those art classes where the teacher builds respect for serious art endeavor, where excessive talking and socializing are minimized, the student's performance and resulting products are of a higher caliber than those of students in a highly permissive situation.

Color plays a very important part in establishing the spirit
or mood of a painting. In this actual-size tempera painting by
an eighth-grade student from West Berlin, Germany, the
colors are subtly neutralized, complementing each other, yet
dominated by the warmth of the reds, browns, and golds. Note
how every varied fish, like a jig-saw puzzle, fits into the next.

33

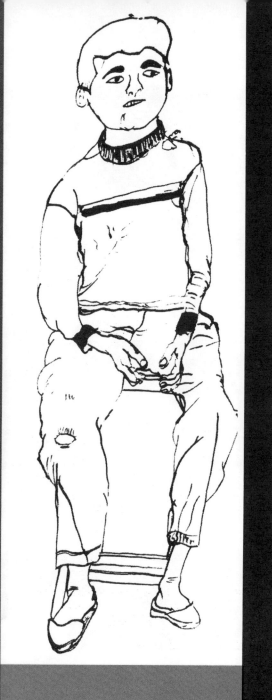

6

EVALUATIVE STRATEGIES

Perhaps the most common and most repeated question that art teachers ask is: How can I help those students who rush through their projects, who resort so easily to exclaiming "I'm finished!" when they have barely begun to tap their resources? Yet the foundation and character of a qualitative art program for adolescents depends basically on how the teacher meets this particular challenge. There is no single formula, no sure-fire panacea for dealing with the student whose interest span is minimal, whose preparation in art is deficient, or whose self-motivation is nil. Each strategy, each approach, each suggestion by the teacher will vary depending upon the student's background, personality, ability and readiness. Some youngsters need general encouragement; some, specific help; others need only a clue; but all of them are entitled to more than vague generalizations. The best evaluative criticisms provide the student with the kind of information he can understand, store, and use over and over again in succeeding projects.

Recommended suggestions that many teachers have found helpful follow.

On line drawings and preliminary linear sketches:

Vary the line from thin to thick for interest.
Vary the pressure of the drawing tool to achieve variety in line.
Vary the line on opposite sides of shape, for example, heavier on one side of a tree trunk, lighter on the other.
Avoid floating lines in delineating the shapes. Carry a line to a meeting with another line. For example, draw veins that touch the edge of the leaf.
Draw what you see, not what you think you see.
Draw slowly and deliberately.

On composition and structure:

Vary the sizes and shapes of objects in your composition.
Avoid mechanically ruled or purely geometric shapes, except in pure design.
Be wary of placing one large or bold object exactly in the center of your composition.
Utilize informal balance for interesting break-up of space.
Add interest to the foreground by placing objects or forms at different levels.
Create interest in the background by varying heights of objects or forms.

Opposite Page—Youngsters who take time to draw their classmates in contour line often emphasize the unique qualities of the model—the honesty, the directness, and the awkwardness of youth caught between childhood and adulthood. These interpretations are by Japanese middle school children.

Provide avenues that lead the eye into the composition by
drawing some objects or shapes that are intersected by
the boundary of the picture plane.

Use overlapping shapes to create unity and shallow space.

Be careful so that two interesting overlapping shapes do
not produce one that is less varied.

Contrast dark areas against light ones, and try patterned
or textured areas against plain or quiet ones for added
interest.

Make the negative space, the space between objects, an
important, varied part of your composition.

On using color and paint:

Limit your color palette. Try using one color in all its
shades and tints, plus black, white and gray.

Neutralize or dull the colors used in a composition.

Use a modified color harmony. Try analogous colors, those
that are adjacent to each other on the color wheel.

Learn to recognize the neutralized colors in your paints,
crayons or pastels such as: umber, ochre, earth green,
sienna brown.

Repeat colors in varying amounts and shapes throughout
your composition to achieve unity. If possible, change
the intensity of the color slightly each time it is
repeated.

Remember that bright, intensive colors attract attention.
Use them for emphasis.

Avoid using bright colors in areas you want subordinated
or subdued.

Use pressure on your crayon or oil pastel to achieve rich,
glowing color.

Be brave in your use of colors. Do not be dominated by
the local color in things. Tree trunks are not always
brown, the leaves are not always green, the sky is not
always blue.

Choose colors for their effectiveness and mood in your
composition and not because "that's the way it was."

If there exists *a single constant factor* in the continuing evaluation and predictable success of the adolescent's art product, it must certainly be the *element of variety* whether it be line, shape, form, value, color, texture or pattern. A study of the great art of the past emphasizes and illuminates again and again the artist's concern with variety in some aspect or another. It is indeed *the spice of art*.

Effective procedures for meeting and dismissing class and for routine tasks will aid in expediting the program, but it is in the area of studio activity and student performance that art-teaching strategy is most vital. Concentration is the key to qualitative work in art, and the teacher must use whatever means he can command to establish a classroom atmosphere in which the youngsters can become seriously involved in their effort without debilitating distractions.

The subtle strategies of high-calibre teaching lie in the words, the sincerity and the confidence a teacher uses when he helps his students evaluate their performance. What he says, how he says it, when he says it, how much he says, what he doesn't say—all are important keys to the successful critique and, consequently, to the completed work. Evaluative clues and admonitions are seldom emphasized in the teacher preparation courses today and, as a result, the young adolescents in the schools are cheated. They rush from *instant* drawing to *instant* coloring without a single challenge by the teacher to examine their work in terms of design, composition or structure.

Note how variety of shape, value, and pattern play a dominant role in the success of these three collages. Repetition of elements helps to unify each composition. Top—University School, Oshkosh. Center—University School, Kalamazoo. Bottom—Savannah Junior High School, Savannah, Georgia.

37

The teacher should have on hand a number of mounts or mats in assorted sizes so that in evaluating the final stages of a student's work, it can be temporarily framed to give it importance and emphasis, thus permitting both student and teacher to appraise it more effectively.

Specifically, one of the more difficult evaluative tasks the teacher must perform is the periodic grading of students. In a content field that is so subjective, so often based on individual expression, and where many interpretations are acceptable, the problem is compounded. Reporting of student progress varies from school to school, some utilizing separate evaluations for behavior and for performance, some simply indicating that the student has performed satisfactorily or unsatisfactorily. The majority of report cards in the junior high school utilize the letter-grade system.

Where only one letter or numerical grade for art is given, teachers often take into account the student's class behavior and working habits as a factor in their evaluation. This procedure may be questioned by some educators, but if the students have been forewarned that their conduct and manners in class will influence their grade, such a course of action is realistic. In almost every instance, wise and economic use of class time by the adolescent results in better performance and more qualitative production.

As far as the evaluation or grading of the specific art products, this task should not prove a difficult one if the students are advised in advance what some of the expectations are. In the project approach recommended for best results, the teacher discusses with the students the possible objectives of the project or assignment. For greater emphasis, he may write these objectives on the blackboard, on a specially prepared chart, or he may even ask the students to take notes. The suggestions or queries may deal with composition, structure, color orchestration, fullest use of the media or technique, or exploitation of processes unique to the project and similar learnings. To be specific, if the students are engaged in a *crayon engraving,* for example, the following self-evaluative questions might be considered:

Did I use enough pressure in applying the crayon to the white construction or drawing paper so that it is solidly covered?

Did I use enough newspaper padding under my paper so that the crayon applied smoothly and evenly?

Did I vary the sizes and shapes of the many crayoned areas?

Did I utilize many hues and values of crayon colors for interest and contrast?

Did I brush off loose flecks of crayon before applying the slightly water-diluted black tempera?

Did I paint the tempera evenly over the crayoned paper, remembering to add a little liquid soap to the tempera to make it adhere to the crayon surface?

Did I wait for the tempera paint to dry thoroughly before beginning the actual engraving?

Does my preliminary composition for the engraving fill the space effectively?

Have I achieved a variety of lines and shapes?

*Opposite Page—The crayon engraving technique embellished with oil pastel passages is adaptable to a wealth of varied subject matter. Top Left—*Still Life, *Danielsville, Georgia. Top Right—*Industrial Scene, *Savannah, Georgia. Lower Left and Right—*Imaginative Theme, *Athens, Georgia, before and after addition of oil pastel.*

Have I broken up the background and foreground successfully?

Have I emphasized varied textures and patterns which are especially exciting in the engraving process?

Did I engrave the basic lines and contours first? Did I utilize the engraving tool (nail, compass point, sloyd knife, pin, etc.) to create a varied, sensitive line?

Did I take the time to engrave characteristic and rich textures, or unique and varied patterns?

Did I create some sharp value contrasts by revealing some underlying crayon shapes as strong highlights?

Have I created a successful dark and light composition, balancing all three possibilities: engraved line alone, textured and patterned delineations, and scraped-out bright crayon shapes?

Did I enrich the composition further by application of oil pastels?

Did I repeat the oil pastel colors for unity?

Did I engrave lines, textures or pattern through the pastel areas for even richer embellishment?

Did I discover some new mixed media possibilities in the process?

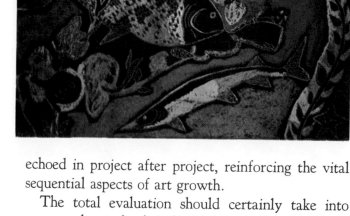

This type of evaluative format can be effectively programmed in every project the student encounters, in order to give purpose, continuity, and direction to the youngster's efforts. Naturally the objectives regarding the technique or process will vary with the specific projects involved, but the important recurring evaluations dealing with the fundamental art concepts of composition, design, structure and form will be echoed in project after project, reinforcing the vital sequential aspects of art growth.

The total evaluation should certainly take into account the student's individual expression, his imaginative and inventive capacity, his rich response to visual stimulation, and the insight he demonstrates in interpreting his impressions, giving aesthetic form to his ideas.

Above—Crayon engravings based on museum sketches. Opposite Page, Top—Student inspired by "still-life" arrangement applying tempera in the preliminary step of a tempera-India ink batik. Bottom—Oil pastel on colored construction paper. Joint venture culminating in a frieze of musicians to enhance one wall of the art room.

7

PLANNING THE PROGRAM

Art is taught in almost every junior high school in this nation, yet it is probably the most inconsistently planned and implemented subject area in the curriculum. In one region the program emphasizes crafts; in another painting, printmaking and sculpture predominate; and in still another correlation with other subjects in the school is stressed. Sometimes there is a token study of art appreciation. The curricular structure differs from country to country, from state to state, from city to city, and even from school to school in the same community. In many instances the teacher's own area of creative competence is the decisive factor in the kind of program offered. In too many communities the junior high art program is merely a continuation of the permissive, free-expression activities practiced in so many elementary schools without any significant change in content or goals. If art in the junior high school is to become a vital, educational force, if it is to become recognized as a serious and justifiable area of growth, then, like any other subject now required, it must have purpose, structure, and content, and it must emphasize the qualitative rather than the quantitative.

Part of the dilemma inherent in planning a qualitative program of art for the junior high youngster stems from the fact that the students come from a variety of elementary schools, each with a different preparation for and predisposition to art. Some come from private schools where art is taught in depth, some from graded schools where art is a brief Friday afternoon activity in coloring or perhaps pasting, and still others come from laissez faire, permissive situations where anything goes in art so long as it goes quickly. Consequently, the teacher of matriculating junior high school students has a singular responsibility. Among other things, he must discover where the incoming youngsters stand in art know-how; he must plan and expedite introductory projects that encourage rather than discourage the self-conscious student; he must introduce the majority of his students to the fundamentals of drawing, designing and composition; he must be able to demonstrate a host of expressive techniques to capture the interest and imagination of the young teenager; and he must give continuity and substance to the varied projects through a constant reference to the language and vocabulary of art.

Opposite Page—Involvement in-depth is an important factor in qualitative performance. This torn-paper collage by a ninth-grade girl from Kagoshima, Japan exemplifies the awareness, patience, and skill a youngster can develop to produce a work of sensitive beauty. The scene is Sakurajima, a lovely cherry-tree garden within the sight of a volcanic mountain.

A realistic junior high school art curriculum should be structured as much as possible around the interests and the needs of the young adolescent, but to a greater degree it should introduce the student to wider horizons and provide broader challenges. The planned program should be amenable enough to allow for the introduction of the topical and the current, but it should shun the instantaneous, the trite, the stereotyped, the expedient and the flashy.

Before the school year begins, the art teacher should outline a program of experiences which he believes will ensure continuing growth in perception, design awareness, problem solving, self-discovery, appreciation and visual literacy. He should also make provisions for the inclusion of free-choice activities during the school term.

Junior high school students should have some opportunities for free-wheeling experimentation, chances to manipulate and make discoveries about colors, papers, tools and three-dimensional materials without the pressure of making a resolved or finished statement, but they should also be challenged with the growing responsibility of carrying projects to completion with all the adjustments, frustrations and choices along the way. The complex composition of a multi-figure drawing, a multi-level still-life arrangement, a field trip to paint a landscape or cityscape, or the building of sculpture or relief should be part of their growing through art. Film making, painting to music and other free-expression activities may be programmed occasionally to vary the fare.

Teachers who include "still-life" drawing and painting in the art program discover it opens many doors to new and unique appreciations for their students. Left—A complex composition, 18" × 24", by an eighth-grade Iowa City youngster exemplifying again the quality achieved by in-depth involvement plus a growing knowledge of water-color techniques.

Continuity or carry-over in art learnings from one project to another must be identified, emphasized and constantly reinforced if it is to be a working factor in the student's art growth. The teacher must direct the youngster's attention to those art principles that unite and give quality to all their endeavors, to the common denominators of art design in the varied things they do. Projects as dissimilar as plaster sculpture, linoleum prints, photography or scrap collage can be linked by stressing art concepts common to all of them. Students should not feel that new standards or new aesthetic evaluations must be developed for each succeeding technique or lesson.

Experienced teachers know that the exploitation of new materials or new-found techniques is often a minor factor in the success of an art project. Legions of tasteless and trite pictures have been painted with the new acrylics, and the latest multi-media technique straight from the art convention floor cannot redeem a single stereotyped composition. On the other hand, teachers and students are constantly and pleasantly surprised by what ordinary crayon or pastels on colored construction paper can produce when the visual inspiration is strong and the effort is characterized by artistic, in-depth involvement.

The teacher who can guide a class of thirty or more students four or more periods a day when each youngster is working on his own choice of material, his own subject matter, and at his own rate of speed, and who still can come up with qualitative results, is a rare

---

Adolescents are intrigued by new materials and new processes. Top—Oconee County Schools, Georgia. A felled tree suggests possibilities for a playground sculpture. Center—Iowa City, Iowa. Lamp craft by gluing tissue paper to inflated balloons. Bottom—Osaka, Japan. Adolescents use lighted sticks to burn varied shaped holes in their abstract tempera color designs.

45

individual indeed. For the majority of teachers in the typically crowded art classes of the junior high school, the *project approach,* in which the entire class engages in the same activity, is definitely recommended as the most practical, most tenable, most economical and most successful procedure. Its many advantages outweigh the disadvantages as any experienced teacher will attest. Utilizing the project method, the teacher can concentrate his strategy on one presentation and one technique rather than on multiple ones. The motivational suggestions and devices can be directed toward common goals; the materials and tools can be organized and distributed more effectively; students engaged in the same technique can learn much from each other; and finally, performance can be evaluated much more expeditiously because the project's technical objectives are common ones.

Critics of project teaching cite the uniformity of expression that occurs when a class engages in the same technique. Naturally a similarity is evident because the materials are similar, the technique is similar and sometimes the subject matter is similar. But in a creative teaching situation, even with the project approach, no two completed works will look exactly alike because no two youngsters are exactly alike. If the program is well planned, every student will have a chance to work in several techniques, several processes during the school term, and may find one he wishes to emphasize in his future elective art classes or as a life's hobby.

Three completed collages by seventh-grade students, Clarke County Junior High, Athens, Georgia, utilizing the project approach. Although the same visual stimulus was provided by the teacher and similar materials were used, no two compositions in the crowded class of youngsters were alike.

Much of the content of adolescent art can be based on the personal preferences of the young adolescent, but the teacher must be prepared to discourage, if possible, the sentimentalized, stereotyped versions of pirouetting ballerinas, prancing horses, smoking gangsters, copies of cartoon characters, snow-capped mountain peaks, palm tree landscapes and Oriental sailing boats. To counteract the students' reliance on the banal and the trite, the teacher should be ready with an arsenal of immediate and viable motivations:

The School Cafeteria at Lunchtime	The School Dance
	The Locker Room
The School Kitchen Staff at Work	The School Maintenance Shop
The Cheerleading Team	The School Picnic
The Science Lab	The Basketball Game
The Art Room	The Homecoming Queen and Court
The Track Meet	
The School Band	Activity Between Classes
The School Combo	Waiting for the School Bus
The School Bicycle Rack	On the School Bus
The Wrestling Team	A View of the School
The School Playground	A Holiday Program
The School Assembly Program	Building a Homecoming Float
The Football Game	The Homecoming Parade
The Marching Band	The Pep Fest
The Gymnastic Team	A View from the School Window
The Baton Twirlers	
The School Swimming Pool	The School Picnic

In these expressions of immediate and familiar activities, the young adolescent's interest and knowledge helps him create a more rewarding interpretation. Top—Tempera. Athens, Georgia. Center—Chalk pastel from posed model. Iowa City. Bottom—Oil pastel from posed model. Danielsville, Georgia.

47

In summary, the following guidelines are suggested for the teacher in planning the middle or junior high school art program.

Schedule an early orientation session to elicit information about the student, his art preparation and potential.

Plan an initial project in which the majority of students can find a measure of success. If possible, introduce an art process that has not been over-exposed in the elementary grades.

Alternate two-dimensional experiences with three-dimensional activities to whet interest.

Plan projects that introduce students to the world of line, shape, form, value, color, texture, pattern, space and time-sequence as working elements in their creative endeavors.

Include techniques which involve the use of complex tools and complex processes.

In most cases, challenge students to draw their inspiration from observed rather than imagined sources, but do not discount the fantastic or the imaginative—for example, the space world of the future.

In typical situations where classes are large and space limited, utilize the project method as a teaching strategy.

In all projects endeavor to make the students aware of their art heritage, of the many faces of art, through a judicious and rich utilization of art books, color slides, films, and reproductions.

Top and Bottom—The world of space intrigues the growing adolescent. Students from a middle school in Tokyo, Japan have invented a fantastic, imaginative future. Medium: colored inks. 18″ × 24″. Center—Group project by youngsters, ages 12–14, Scotland. Reproduced by courtesy of London Sunday Mirror.

48

8

A RECOMMENDED PROGRAM

The selected techniques and the sequence of art experiences recommended in this guide are the result of many years of in-depth teaching by the authors, of continuous experimentation, of materials and media exploration, of process and product evaluation and of direct observation of middle school art in a number of countries in order to discover what young adolescents respond to, what can serve as a foundation for their continuing art interest, what they can become *deeply* involved in, what can increase their perceptual awareness, what can add to their aesthetic discrimination, and what can help them understand and appreciate their art heritage.

Young adolescents express a common desire to grow in drawing and related graphic or representational skills. They look to the teacher for support and for guidance. However, drawing is perhaps the most misunderstood, the most neglected area in the entire art program. Naturally, students should not be forced into complex drawing assignments without some preliminary orientation. Much depends on their elementary school drawing experiences and their own native ability to record ideas graphically.

Instead of a smorgasbord of unrelated single-period activities, the art program for the young adolescent should be planned for in-depth involvement and sequential growth. After an initial multi-theme collage project which can provide each youngster with an opportunity for a successful performance, thus building his confidence, the teacher can gradually introduce fundamental drawing and design techniques. Projects involving contour line, ink line and wash, gesture drawing, value, color, pattern, texture and creative lettering are recommended to build a foundation necessary for sequential art growth in grades six, seven, eight, and nine.

A measure of confidence in working with line and value should be established before the young adolescent tackles the intricacies of color orchestration. Students who may be successful in linear expression often need special guidance when faced with color choices and color manipulation.

Coloring and painting skills may be developed to some extent through the exploration of various media.

Opposite Page—This sensitive pen-and-ink drawing by a young Japanese girl of thirteen is evidence of an in-depth art program in action. Two hours of studio art experiences per week are required for children in grades 1 through 8 in Japanese schools.

51

The popular wax crayon or the new oil pastel on colored construction paper or colored railroad board still has undiscovered possibilities. Mixed media, too, have opened up new avenues of color expression. Colored tissue paper and ink line collages, crayon and watercolor resists, and tempera and India ink batiks are all popular with adolescents. Crayon and multi-crayon engraving which often can be enhanced by a final enrichment with oil pastels offer new directions in color for the student.

Then there is the challenging, exciting area of printmaking. Linoleum prints, monoprints, reduction prints, woodblocks, collographs and paper or celluloid engraving—all have universal appeal for the adolescent.

And finally there are the important and popular experiences in three-dimensional design: sculpture in plaster, clay, sandstone, lava rock, paraffin, foamglass and wood; constructions in paper, wire, metal, wood and "found" materials; and the craft experiences in pottery, weaving, stitchery, plaster relief, mosaics and jewelry. Qualified teachers can offer experiences in photography and film making if the budget allows for **them**

The history and appreciation of art along with art criticism can be a significant part of every junior high school program if the teacher has the budget for, or access to, quality art reproductions, color slides, film-strips, films or artifacts. Each project can begin with

Everyday, immediate resources are the teachers most success-ful arsenal for rich motivation. Top—A bicycle is commonly available. Manchester, England. Center—A stationwagon with all doors open. Oshkosh, Wisconsin. Bottom—A class-mate across the table. Iowa City, Iowa.

a visual presentation and discussion of related efforts by distinguished professional artists, designers and craftsmen, both past and present. This is why it is so important that the art teacher have a rich college or university background in the history, theory and criticism of art. It is not within the scope of this book to suggest the endless possibilities for art studio and art history correlation, but it is the responsibility of every professionally-minded teacher to acquire the resources he needs to implement this important aspect of a qualitative art program.

The discriminative art teacher is highly selective in programming a curriculum for the junior high school, eschewing those peripheral activities which offer little more than therapy and play. He discovers there are disciplines and experiences in the studio arts that are relatively more important and contribute more significantly to aesthetic, perceptual and appreciative growth than others.

The projects and practices recommended and described in this guide can provide the foundation for a general art course for young adolescents in grades seven, eight or nine. Drawing, designing, collage and painting are basic in any proposed curriculum. Printmaking in its many aspects and the three-dimensional experiences in sculpting, modeling and constructing offer the excitement and challenge of new processes and techniques with new materials that are so very important to the growing youngster.

Top—The art room as a most immediate theme for painting. Keokuk, Iowa. Center—Classmate combo (see students sketching from class models, page 66). University Schools, Oshkosh. Bottom—Mixed-media painting and collage. England. Courtesy of LONDON SUNDAY MIRROR.

53

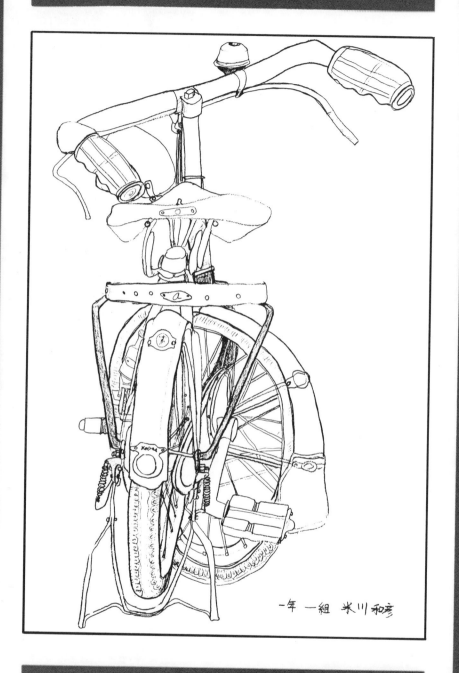

一年 一組 米川和彦

DRAWING

The teaching of drawing to young adolescents is especially difficult in today's permissive art room climate. Yet, drawing taught well gives direction and substance to the purposeful involvement of the youngster in art. In fact, it can be the foundation on which almost every project in the junior high school is developed.

Unfortunately, in too many schools drawing is one of the weakest areas in the whole art program. This situation can be attributed in part to the fact that so many youngsters come to the junior high school with limited preparation or background experiences in drawing practices. Most of their drawing has been the spontaneous "draw-out-of-your-head" or "draw-what-you-want" type and, consequently, they lack confidence in attempting what they now feel is a difficult task. But if the art program is to have any status at all, if the quality of the student's performance is to be enhanced, then the problem of drawing must be faced and resolved.

Drawing is the bane and joy of the art program. Where youngsters are sold on drawing, the teacher is "Home!" If students believe that you believe they can do it, they will do it! Do not underestimate them. Top—Savannah, Georgia. Center—Iowa City, Iowa. Bottom—Kumamoto, Japan.

55

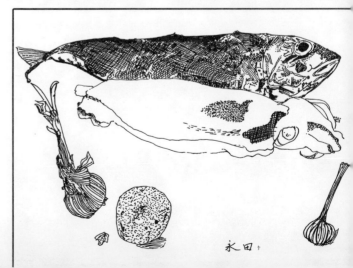

The primary purpose in emphasizing drawing is that it enables the student to increase his latent abilities to perceive and respond. The mental activity implied in seeing goes hand-in-hand with the student's insight as he responds to the myriad of contours and shapes of the objects which constantly meet his eye. The student eventually comes to realize that drawing is actually an extension of seeing.

A very basic requirement in teaching drawing is to help the adolescent develop his *line* language. Line is essentially an artist's tool or invention to express the boundaries of things, where two objects, areas or values meet or overlap. Students should become familiar with the vocabulary of line: weight, mass, variety, emphasis, space, action and direction. The goal most teachers strive for, however, is to have students become *sensitive* to line quality—sensitive to the unlimited potential of line.

There are some effective approaches to help a student who is self-conscious about his drawing ability. To begin with, if the youngster is presented with something stimulating to draw, half the battle is won. A great deal depends on the subject, on visuals that the student can identify with. Sometimes the very immediate, the very ordinary or common object can become the catalyst, the inspiration for a sensitive drawing or painting. In one junior high school in Japan the students drew their own box luncheons in brush and ink. Yet no two were alike. Each was a personal expression. In another school the students drew their own hands in a variety of positions. In still

Drawing begins where the youngsters are—the school parking lot, the playground, even the lunches they bring to school, as these Japanese girls have found. Center—Note the space-saving plastic, collapsible water containers!

another art class the students emptied the contents of their pockets or purses and made an overlapping design of the items. Youngsters in art classes today might draw handbags, baseball gloves, wristwatches, shoes or boots, a coat or sweater hanging from a chair, the teacher's closet, a supply cupboard opened to reveal its contents, the ceramic wheel, the slide projector, or an arrangement of the room's chairs and easels. The best art teachers gradually acquire an assortment of objects that are ideal as subject matter for drawing: animal skulls, bottles, lanterns, potted plants, assorted drapery in various patterns, and nature's gifts of stones, feathers, rocks, seeds, nuts, twigs, leaves, sea shells and coral.

Drawing tools should be chosen for their potential in producing a variety of lines. Pencils, charcoal, Conté crayon, bamboo pens, sticks and thin dowels sharpened to a point are suggested. The common pen and ink have their merits but they are often overshadowed by frustrations caused by dripped or spattered ink. The teacher should discuss possibilities of the various drawing tools.

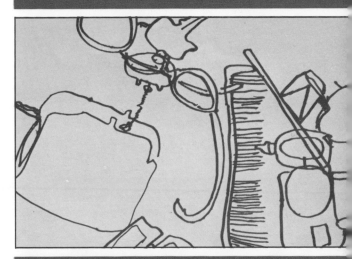

The time and attention allotted to preliminary drawings and compositions is most crucial. The students should never be made to feel they are being rushed through the drawing phase. This is the stage where the teacher faces his most critical test because it is what he says here, what he approves, what changes he suggests during these initial drawing periods that can make the difference between results that are merely adequate or average and those that are outstanding.

More immediate ideas for drawing and painting. Top—Student's wristwatch. England. Courtesy of London Sunday Mirror. *Center—Contents of pocket or purse. Oshkosh, Wisconsin. Bottom—Office typewriter. England. Courtesy of* London Sunday Mirror.

57

CONTOUR DRAWING

The contour method of drawing, where hand and eye must be in gear when the drawing takes place, has been generally accepted by junior high school teachers as a valid and qualified approach to the mastery of graphic expression by young adolescents. Although it demands total involvement, insight and intense empathic response, its rewards are inherent more often in the process than in the results. Yet the artistic impact of contour line and the resulting composition can be very qualitative, indeed.

For the youngster, the contour-drawing method can sometimes be discouraging and physically exhausting unless it is presented in understandable stages. Results are often disappointing at first since the visual statement does not resemble the familiar image the student is accustomed to. In order to free the adolescent from his concern over the initial efforts, it is necessary to explain that realistic rendering is not of prime importance.

There is beauty in "blind contour" drawing if it is done conscientiously. Suggest that students do not look at their paper except at critical stages and honestly let their eye prompt their hand where to move.

In the initial drawing session, the teacher might ask the students to pretend their finger is the drawing tool and to follow the contour of the object on the paper without actually making a mark. Continued practice is necessary to deaccelerate the tendency of students to scan quickly.

For contour practice sessions or short exercises, it is suggested that all students in the class begin drawing at the same time and on the same problem. Students new to the contour method should begin with simple objects such as a fruit or a bottle. After several such studies they can be assigned more complex configurations that will enable them to grow in handling overlapping forms, pattern, and compositional space.

Everyday objects make eye-opening and visually exciting material for contour drawing. These may include bicycles, motorcycles, farm machinery, trucks, car motors, clocks, coffee grinders, electric fans, typewriters, meat grinders, apple corers, old telephones, tea pots, antique sewing machines, bird cages, old shoes, kerosene cans, jugs, animal traps, egg beaters, lawn mowers, corn shellers, musical instruments, lanterns, milk cans, kettles, old steam irons, sea shells, driftwood, antlers, and gourds.

In blind contour drawing the student looks intently at the object and draws its contours or edges without looking at his paper. He should be reminded not to let his eye move faster than his drawing tool. When he is drawing complex subject matter, he may depart from the blind approach at critical junctures, look at the object and reposition his drawing tool on the paper.

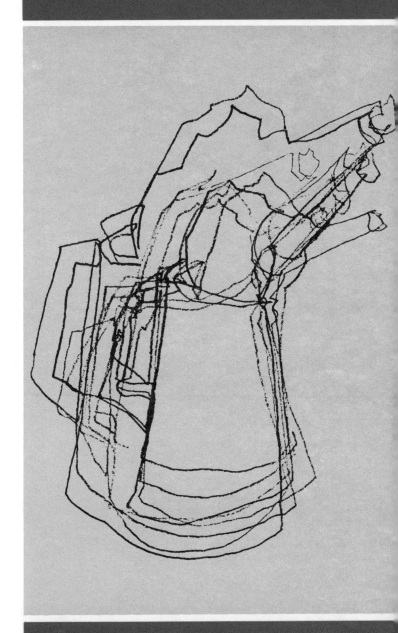

In teaching contour drawing to young adolescents, begin with single, simple objects and proceed gradually to more complex arrangements. Contour study (grade 7). Iowa City, Iowa.

59

山内康敬

In his first attempts at contour delineation, the student should be instructed to press very hard with the pencil and to draw very, very slowly. He should be cautioned against erasing lines and should be encouraged to draw a second or third line if he wishes to correct an unsatisfactory first effort.

Drawing tools suggested for the contour approach include ball point, felt or nylon-tipped pens and similar linear markers that produce an uninterrupted flow of line. Drawing with an ink-filled stick or bamboo pen and allowing it to run completely dry before refilling produces a unique wet-to-dry line. If the drawing ink is permanent in nature, watercolor washes in a limited palette can extend the drawing process into painting. The common drawing or sketching pencil, preferably in a semi-soft lead, is perhaps the most effective medium for contour mastery because it allows the youngster to concentrate all his efforts on the drawing without worrying about ink spillage or ink shortage.

After concentrated practice in the contour method with simple, inanimate objects, the students can progress to figure drawing and more elaborate genré.

60

When "contour" becomes "a way of drawing" for the young
adolescent, he can move confidently to more demanding subjects, as this very sensitive and personal interpretation by a
twelve-year-old Japanese girl of her room proves. Notice especially her doll collection in its glass case.

61

DRAWING: THE PORTRAIT

One of the most effective, dependable and immediate sources for expressive drawings in the junior high school art repertoire is the adolescent himself. The self-portrait or portrait of a classmate should certainly be on the agenda of any realistically planned program.

Suggested motivations for the portrait-drawing project should include a visual presentation of color slides, films and reproductions that reveal different styles and techniques of portraiture as expressed by noted artists, past and present. Students might be shown portrait studies by Leonardo da Vinci, Albrecht Durer, Hans Holbein, Rembrandt van Rijn, Jan Vermeer, Diego Velasquez, Edgar Degas, Henri Matisse, Vincent Van Gogh, Amadeo Modigliani, Pablo Picasso, George Bellows, Ben Shahn, or Mauricio Lasansky.

Skill in drawing has helped this young English boy produce a portrait that is expressive, vital, and unique. The hands and arms serve as counterpoints and bring excitement ·to what might otherwise be a pedestrian pose. Note variety and sensitivity of line. Courtesy of LONDON SUNDAY MIRROR.

In projects involving the drawing of the portrait, one of the teacher's major responsibilities is to divert the student from a reliance on the typical portrait stereotype: the stiff symmetrical frontal pose, the square shoulders, the rigidly measured features. To begin with, time and care should be taken in posing the model, if it is a classmate, so that a more informal and exciting composition will result.

Arms and hands can be utilized as effective contrasts or counterpoints in the total composition. Assorted objects to hold or manipulate can be acquired. Some suggested poses are: holding or playing a musical instrument, holding or carrying sports equipment, putting on a hat, scarf or helmet, combing or brushing the hair, holding an open umbrella, putting on make-up, reading a book, straddling a chair with head resting on folded arms, or arms folded above the head. The utilization of the three-quarter or full profile should also be considered. Sometimes the background against which the model or student poses can add immeasurably to the total composition. A youngster posed against a multi-paned window, against a giant poster, or in combination with a still-life arrangement suggests many possibilities.

Portrait stereotypes are usually the result of superficial observation which leads to superficial drawing. If the teacher can somehow bring the students to look intently at the model, whether it be their own image in a mirror or a classmate posing in front of them, to pay attention to his or her unique characteristics, then a giant step is made toward qualitative portraiture.

This superb contour drawing from a junior high school exhibit in San Francisco has many of the qualities of fine art— restraint, simplicity, directness, technical virtuosity, and presence.

64

Drawings by young adolescents. Bottom Center—Oshkosh, Wisconsin. Bottom Right—Charcoal drawing. Lighter areas achieved by erasing with kneaded eraser or art gum. Pattie Hillsman Junior High, Athens, Georgia. Bottom Left—Terrell High School, Atlanta. Top Right—Osaka, Japan. Top Center and Left—University Schools, Iowa City.

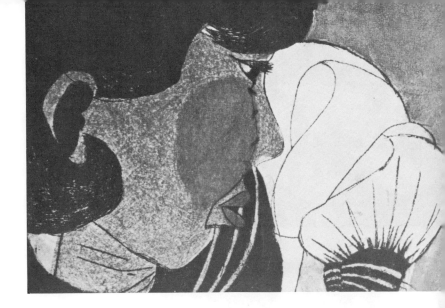

Guide the youngsters to use the contour-drawing approach for maximum delineation. Suggest that in most instances they begin by drawing the head first, drawing it large enough so that the entire portrait will fill the paper space effectively. Remind them that the strategic placement of the head on the page is vital to the final resolution of the composition. In most cases this means they ought to draw the head near the top of their paper rather than in the middle of it.

Encourage awareness. Ask them to note the size of the neck in relation to the head, the way the neck curves subtly into the shoulders, the change in the size of the arms from shoulder to elbow, from elbow to wrist. Ask them to place their open hand over their face to realize its size in relation to the head. Discuss characteristic shapes of the head, how it changes from chin to cheek, from cheek to brow. Call attention to the hair line, how the hair follows the contour of the head. Discuss the shape and juncture of the ears to the head, the possibilities of delineating the nose, the lips as two subtly differing forms, and the importance of the eyelids as characteristic elements. Through questioning bring out the fact that no two people, no two faces are exactly alike and, furthermore, that even the two sides of a person's face are not exactly the same.

If the youngsters are concerned that their drawing does not look like the model, tell them the aim of expressive portraiture is not to achieve a photographic likeness but to try to capture the spirit or character of the subject, that the same model drawn by different artists would appear different in each rendition.

Top—A sensitive drawing by a Japanese youngster. Courtesy of Sakura Craypas Company. Bottom—A well composed and unusual drawing of a youngster with a transparent umbrella. England. Courtesy of LONDON SUNDAY MIRROR.

Because the young adolescent often has difficulty in drawing the model's apparel, he must be guided to pay careful attention to the fact that the lines or borders of collars, sleeves, cuffs, head bands, hats, skirts, bracelets, wristwatches, belts, and socks *curve around* the body's forms. Seams, wrinkles and folds in the model's clothing should be observed and drawn deliberately and sensitively, and in most cases these delineative lines should terminate at another juncture rather than float on the surface. Patterns in clothing, especially stripes, checks and plaids should be drawn to follow the curves of the body and to change with the contours. The key to successful results is careful observation.

Young adolescents are sensitive to differences in each other, to changes in their own physical growth. A portrait drawing could be the most meaningful way of capitalizing on their growing interest in themselves and their classmates. But the project must be handled with tact and discretion. Be prepared for the occasional self-conscious tittering or embarrassed laughter when a student shows his classmate the portrait he did of him. Be understanding when a student does not want to model for his classmates. There are always a number of volunteers. The student's first struggling efforts should not discourage the teacher or the student. In a situation where the youngsters are using their time economically, observing the model carefully and growing in drawing skills day to day, their creative expression will be a testimony to their involvement.

Top—A football player modeling for eighth-grade art class. Students drew him in several positions, and then selected several drawings to build a composition for a painting. (See picture, page 47.) Center and Bottom—Art class in action. University School, Oshkosh, Wisconsin.

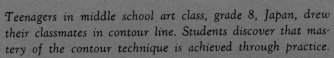

Teenagers in middle school art class, grade 8, Japan, drew their classmates in contour line. Students discover that mastery of the contour technique is achieved through practice.

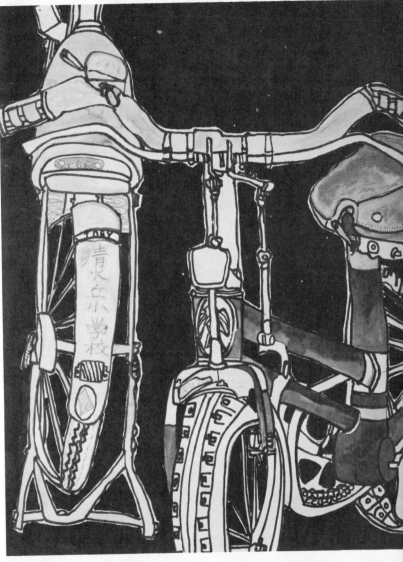

Adolescents and their characteristic interests are rich sources for art project motivation as the illustrations on this and opposite page prove.

It is important that the adolescent have rich visual stimulation in order to do quality work. Here in the art room of the University School, Oshkosh, Wisconsin, co-author David Hodge has provided an ever-changing environment for the youngsters to draw. Students model in unusual gear surrounded by a panoply of intriguing Americana. The resulting drawings by the youngsters on this page and elsewhere in the text justify the time and effort expended by both teacher and student.

These multi-figure paintings indicate that the young adolescent has spent much time in planning his composition. In some instances, different students take turns modeling, and the student draws them one at a time, overlapping figures as he proceeds, avoiding a monotony of heights or postures. In other approaches, the student draws his classmates as they are seated before him in class. Each method has merits. On occasion, the youngsters may draw from memory or recall.

The teacher should be constantly searching for the unusual
treasure to share with his students. A corner of the art room
transformed into a continuing resource center for drawing,
painting, and printmaking ideas.

DRAWING: THE STILL LIFE

The most successful art teachers in the junior high or middle school find it both expedient and critically resourceful to have on hand a variety of interesting objects, man-made items and nature's gifts, that the student can refer to as subject material for drawing, either for sketching practice or for preliminary compositions leading to paintings, prints, collages and mixed media interpretations.

Apart from the occasionally scheduled field trip to a sketching site, the sensitively planned still-life arrangement provides the most immediate, the most effective and the most reliable motivational arsenal the teacher has at his command.

A "still-life" arrangement should be organized with an artist's sensitivity—contrasting shape against shape, dark value against light value, patterned area against quiet area.

73

If utilized to the fullest degree, it can prove a significant strategy in the teaching of basic compositional and design concepts, especially the creation of shallow space, exciting positive and negative space discoveries, and the diverse utilization of foreground and background areas. A corollary dividend of the project is the renewed interest and sensitivity that youngsters often develop for ordinary, everyday objects especially when they are guided to note their unique design qualities and learn to translate them into graphic imagery.

The arrangement of the still life can be a cooperative adventure for both student and teacher in which the fundamental assets of a challenging composition should be incorporated: variety of shapes and forms, plain and intricate, tall and short, and a variety of levels on which the objects rest, including, of course, those aspects such as drapery and table coverings that give unity to the ensemble. Arrange the still life in a location where the majority of the students can view it effectively. Sometimes this means putting it in the center of the room with the students in a circle around it. Move desks and drawing tables when necessary. Usually the more objects there are in a still life and the more complex the arrangement, the greater opportunity the young adolescents have for compositional success. As in all creative undertakings, no two still-life interpretations will be alike even though the youngsters work from the same arrangements.

A "still-life" arrangement becomes the point of departure for rich expression in color, shape, pattern, and structure. Tempera paintings. Pattie Hillsman Junior High, Athens, Georgia.

74

Another colorful example proving that an exciting "still-life" arrangement inspires youngsters toward qualitative effort. Oil pastel on 9" x 12" colored construction paper. Grade seven. Clarke County Junior High School, Athens, Georgia.

NANCY
WALLACE

There are countless possibilities for arranging a classroom "still life," as the illustrations above suggest. Opposite Page— Contour drawing of "still-life" (grade 8). Iowa City, Iowa.

A highly sensitive and expressive drawing inspired by on-the-site seeing and sketching, plus artistic imagination and license to simplify, distort, and rearrange the visual elements to create unity and mood. Note especially how the preliminary ink washes tie the composition together. Notice, too, the variety in line, in the shapes and positions of the houses, in the windows and roofs, and in overlapping forms. Finally, note how the houses, trees, and clouds terminated at the boundary of the composition create avenues leading the observer into the picture. Actual size. Dubuque, Iowa.

DRAWING: THE LANDSCAPE

The majority of problems encountered by teacher and student on drawing or sketching field trips can be resolved by effective planning beforehand. The teacher should first check out possible sketch sites. Permission to be away from school should be cleared with the principal's office and, when necessary, signed permission slips should be obtained from parents. Arrangements for the use of the school bus or other transportation should be made in advance.

On the day of the field trip, the teacher should review rules of behavior for such excursions and remember to caution students about respecting private property in the sketching vicinity. Directions for proceeding to and returning from the field site should be clear. Keep the class in a group, bringing up stragglers when necessary. Appoint responsible monitors. If roads or highways are to be crossed, stop signs to be held by monitors to warn and halt motor traffic are recommended.

A view of Kyoto by a middle school student from Japan. Notice the bold approach achieved with the blunt felt-tip marker. Also note the effective balance of patterned roof tiles against plain areas, and the subtle depth achieved through overlapping forms without overt reliance on formal perspective principles.

79

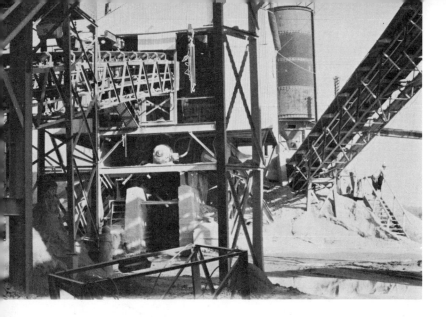

In most instances materials and supplies for drawing or sketching should be distributed to the class before leaving the art room. Students can carry their own drawing boards if they walk to the site. A recommended drawing board is an 18- by 24-inch piece of beaverboard or Upson board, its edges bound with masking tape. Drawing paper can be stapled or tacked to this type of sketching board. If a bus is used for transportation, class monitors can be responsible for the materials which can be distributed on arrival at the sketching site. The teacher should check to see that there are enough drawing boards and drawing supplies beforehand.

At the sketching site the teacher should discourage students from sitting too close together. An ounce of prevention is worth a pound of cure. As many an experienced teacher can testify, too many field trips have ended up as time-wasting social hours.

The teacher of art should constantly scout for unusual sights to draw. An unusual house, a construction crew at work, a view down an alleyway. Some teachers utilize reference photographs and color slides when a sketching excursion is out of the question. Opposite Page—Paintings by Japanese youngsters. Ikuno Junior High, Osaka, Japan.

Opposite Page—The essence of the contour drawing aesthetic is distilled in this expressive interpretation of a religious cultural treasure shrine on such a field trip. Below—Japanese middle school students go on many sketching excursions to draw temples, shrines, factories, bridges, and harbors.

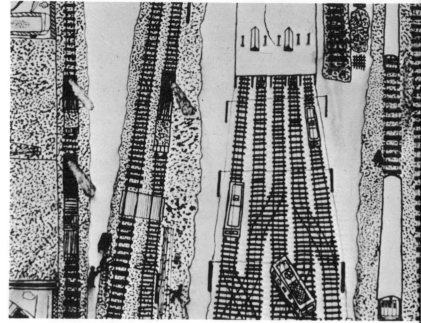

It is folly to take the youngsters to a sketching site and simply say, "Draw!" Young adolescents at this stage need special assistance with their drawings; they sometimes want to know how to begin, what to draw first, what to look for, what details to put in, what to do if they wish to start over again, how to make the sidewalk stay flat, how to make the fence stand up, how to make the steps go back, how to make the porch come out, or how to make the roof tilt. These and a hundred-and-one uncertainties disturb them. The instructor might simply suggest that the student begin drawing the object or shape nearest to him at the bottom of his paper and build from there, or find a shape in the middle of the view he likes, draw that first and then continue to left and right, up and down, or perhaps use a view finder and draw all the shapes as they relate to the frame of the finder. Although the teacher can persist to convince the youngsters that a totally naturalistic rendition is not a criteria of a successful drawing, he still must be able to assist them at those crucial stages of their drawing when mastery of a difficult visual image is important to them.

Left—Growth in drawing comes with practice, as paintings and drawings by Japanese youngsters of everyday themes prove. They are the result of intense perception and awareness, usually derived from sketches drawn at the sight.
Right—Railroad terminal by young Berliner. Pen and ink. Courtesy of Pelikan Company, West Germany.

The most perplexing and possibly the most important responsibility of the art teacher at the sketching site is to guide each student to a self-evaluation of his drawing in terms of improving the composition and the linear quality, of emphasizing characteristic structure and detail, and of delineating space. But in the final essence, if all the teacher did was to bring the youngster to see something he had not really seen before, to notice something he had never noticed until then, to call his attention to a molding on a door frame, a shadow on a wall, the tilt of a telephone pole, the overlapping shape of shingles, the variety in a tree bark or the cornice on a house, he has succeeded in enriching the life of his students because he may have started them on an endless quest of shapes, patterns and color.

Youngsters want to know how to draw. Teachers must develop sufficient confidence to guide them through critical stages. Above—A young adolescent girl used the contour method to capture the essence of dilapidated buildings. Oshkosh, Wisconsin.

85

OIL PASTEL

The potential of a new art medium and the challenge of a novel technique may often be decisive factors in the success of a project. The relatively new oil pastels now on the school art supply market with their exciting range of colors and ease of application have a definite appeal to the young adolescent who likes the rich, painterly effects that they produce.

Oil pastels work especially well on deep-colored construction paper where the color background often serves as a unifying or complementing factor. Although these stick pastels can be used impressionistically, blending or glazing color over color, the students should be encouraged in their first effort with the medium to apply the pastels in solid color areas, keeping contrast of values in mind. Because the intensity of the pastel hues are affected by the paper color, some teachers suggest that the student try out the pastel on the reverse side of his construction paper before using it in his composition.

The vibrant, sensuous colors of oil pastel on colored construction paper positively glow! Opposite Page—The imaginative jungle scene is by a young teenager from Athens, Georgia. Right—The boy on the motorcycle is by a talented adolescent from the Public Schools in Danielsville, Georgia. Student models posed for preliminary sketches.

The following recommendations have been found helpful in oil pastel projects where colored construction paper is utilized for the background:

Make the preliminary sketch or drawing with white chalk or a very light colored pastel. Chalk is excellent because it can be erased easily if the student wishes to make changes.

Apply the pastel colors in solid areas for boldest effects.

Avoid outlining a shape or object in a color that will isolate the object or shape from the rest of the composition.

Apply the color very lightly where you want the color of the paper to create a complementing or contrasting effect.

Avoid scribbling or haphazard application of the pastel.

Remember that although colors may be different in hue, for example red and green, they may be exactly alike in value. Be aware of this when you try to achieve exciting contrasts of value.

Be cognizant of the many tints and shades of a color: dark green, light green, blue-green, yellow-green, dull green, bright green. This awareness is especially important when coloring leaves and grassy fields in all their variety of light and shadow.

The black, white and grey oil pastels can be used quite successfully with any color arrangement. In fact, they may aid in unifying or enriching the composition.

It is important to remember that colors, both tints and shades, bright and dull, should be repeated for unity, but avoid, if possible, repetition of a color in a similar size and shape if a lively variety is desired.

One vital factor in successful color orchestration is that a color or hue repeated to achieve unity should be slightly differentiated in value or intensity so that the echo of the color is there without the monotony of a stereotyped repetition. This admonition is especially true when a student is delineating a pattern such as bricks on a wall, tiles on a roof or stones in a walk, where the repetition of colors could become static and lifeless unless they are subtly and sensitively altered.

Another interpretation of a popular theme by an adolescent student from Danielsville, Georgia. These youngsters were fortunate to have a teacher who helped them to see the many and varied possibilities of the oil pastel technique.

When the number of colors in the oil pastel box is limited, new colors can be achieved by applying one color over another. Students must be guided to do this effectively and should practice combining colors on the back of their paper. The oil pastel, in most cases, is a soft dissolving medium and sometimes only a small pressure of the stick is needed to change the value or intensity of the first color applied. However, in some instances and for some effects, the second color must be applied heavily and sometimes blended with the fingers or facial tissue. A very light color such as white, pink or yellow cannot be altered easily to a dark color by the application of a dark color. The student who desires to change a light pastel shape or segment of his composition to a dark value must remove the light color first with a scraping tool of some sort.

However, other color effects and combinations can be achieved. A green can become blue-green with the application of blue pastel in the desired amount. A green can be dulled or neutralized through the application of red. A green can be lightened with the application of white. Sometimes a shimmering multiple color effect can be achieved by glazing color over color over color. Even black can be slightly changed by the application of white.

Left—One approach in working with oil pastels is illustrated. Eastman, Georgia. Top—The preliminary white chalk drawing on colored construction paper and initial coloring. Center—Additional colors applied and repeated in solid areas to insure strong value contrasts. Bottom—Background colors tie composition together and provide a definite rhythm.

89

To alter a color the student must apply the second color with just enough pressure to effect a change, but not so much pressure that the first layer of color is destroyed. Usually this can be done in controlled directional strokes, softer at first and then with more pressure as needed. In some cases undesirable effects occur when white pastel is applied to a primary color, but these can be modified by glazing over the white layer with another neutralizing color.

Oil pastels can be successfully used in multi-media projects over tempera and crayon and very effectively as a final stage in crayon engraving by applying them over the black tempera areas. Where oil pastel is used on colored railroad board, oaktag or similar glossy surfaced papers, the student may enliven and enrich the composition by engraving or scratching lines, patterns or textures through the pastel coat down to the surface of the paper, and even by scraping away whole areas for contrast. For this type of engraving, assorted nails, finger files or paring knives may be used. A tool especially recommended for this technique, if the budget will allow for it, is the short-bladed and relatively safe Sloyd knife. It can engrave a line that changes from thin to wide and can scrape away whole areas of pastel where needed.

Composition from posed model (grade 8). University School, Oshkosh, Wisconsin. Notice how the placement of the figure against "still-life" arrangement helped the adolescent artist create an interesting background for his pastel painting.

The posed figure becomes a challenging subject for an oil pastel. A sensitive preliminary drawing in white chalk on colored paper was the starting point. Note how the figures fill the space and flow into the boundaries to create entry to the composition. Center—Adolescent girls work on self-portraits within frame of circle. Left and Right—Grade 7. Danielsville, Georgia.

91

MULTI-CRAYON ENGRAVING

Junior high adolescents respond readily to innovative techniques and complex processes. New ways to create with the standard crayon often reactivate their waning interest in this medium which they tend to associate with their childish endeavors. The multi-crayon engraving project offers them the challenge of qualitative involvement in a coloring exploration that is full of surprises and individual discoveries. (For a detailed description of this technique see F. Wachowiak and T. Ramsay, *Emphasis: Art,* International Textbook Co., Scranton, Pa., 1965, pp. 106-108.) The discovery of the potential of railroad board as a background for the overlays of crayon has added a new and exciting dimension to this project. This board, slightly heavier than tagboard but with the same hard, glossy surface, comes in colors of pink, orange, bright green, red, turquoise, yellow, blue and black, which can be exploited beautifully as the background color during the engraving process and adds immensely to the aesthetic quality of the product. It also eliminates the need for the final staining process recommended for oaktag.

Opposite Page—These successful multi-crayon engravings on railroad board are by eighth-grade youngsters. University School, Oshkosh, Wisconsin. Students built up the crayon layers, then referring to their sketch, employed nails, finger files, Sloyd knives, and plastic modeling tools to engrave linear and solid areas. Above—Young girl beginning the engraving process.

Students should be allowed to choose the color they wish for their background paper and encouraged to utilize a multi-crayon application that will ensure an effective contrast against the paper color. Remind them to use the side of the crayon in successive overlays and not to press too hard with the point of the crayon since this tends to destroy the layer of crayon underneath. Applying the crayon with swift, short strokes first in one direction and then in another direction is the most effective method. For engraving a line or scraping away a whole area of crayon, the short-blade sloyd knife is a highly recommended tool.

The following evaluative questions will prove helpful to both teacher and student in the multi-crayon engraving project:

Did the student develop a well-composed preliminary sketch from observation or did he use his imagination to create a design or fantasy motif as a basis for his engraving?

Did he take time and thought to apply the crayons in successive layers, light to dark or dark to light, to achieve a rich and unusual color combination or patina?

Did he successfully exploit the engraving technique by employing a variety of incised lines, patterns and textures?

Did he create effective contrasts between the background paper color and the crayoned areas by removing or scraping away areas, both negative and positive, in various shapes and sizes?

Did he establish a mood or new combinations of colors through experimentation?

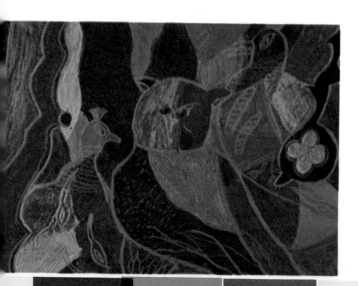

94

The multi-crayon engraving technique lends itself to the interpretation of varied subjects—still life, figure studies, and cityscape or landscape. Any glossy-coated colored paper can be utilized as a background surface. Opposite Page—Students cooperate on segments of a large mural using oil pastel on colored construction paper.

TEMPERA-INDIA INK BATIK

Adolescents are intrigued by new processes in painting. The tempera batik process provides them with a novel approach in using a familiar material and has an additional surprise element built in which makes the technique a favorite one with young teenagers.

The success of a tempera batik, as in all qualitative art projects, depends on rich motivation, a strong, exciting basic composition, and an understanding of the technical process.

Subject matter themes for tempera batiks are unlimited. Exotic birds, butterflies, fish, assorted plants and jungle animals in their tropical habitat provide rich possibilities for varied shapes and intricate patterns of color. Still-life arrangements, complex cityscapes and student models attired in unusual costumes posed against colorfully arranged background are also challenging.

The project begins with a drawing, preferably in contour line with white chalk on a strong semi-rough paper. Heavyweight (80-pound) colored construction paper in colors of pink, orange, yellow, light brown, green or light blue is recommended.

Oatmeal or bogus paper can be utilized if special care is made to avoid tearing it during rinsing process. Suggested sizes of paper for tempera batiks are 12 by 18 inches, 18 by 18 inches or 18 by 24 inches.

It is important that the students make a carefully observed drawing of the subject. Chalk lines should vary in width. This variation will play a key role in the success of the batik. Ordinarily the line composition should fill and even go beyond the boundary of the paper. Details of pattern in feathers, bark, fish scales, veins of leaves, decoration on costumes and similar effect should all be carefully delineated.

These preliminary compositions should be evaluated by both student and teacher for possible improvements before the actual painting begins. Look for varied line quality and shapes, areas of texture and pattern balanced by plain, quiet areas, objects at different levels both in foreground and background, overlapping planes, and a composition that fills the entire page.

Before students paint, the teacher might show the class color slides or films on stained-glass windows, reproductions of paintings by Georges Rouault or Henri Matisse, especially those where the latter utilizes black lines so effectively. These would help the student see the results of brilliant color expression complemented by black outlines and give them a clue to the tempera batik aesthetic.

Liquid tempera in an undiluted state and of a rather thick consistency is best for this technique. Be sure the paint is mixed thoroughly before using it.

Opposite Page—Tempera batik by eighth-grade student. Terrell High School, Atlanta. Teachers who themselves have success with the tempera-India ink technique in college (see page 8) are eager to share it with their students. Youngsters are fascinated by the final rinsing process—they facetiously call the results "washouts."

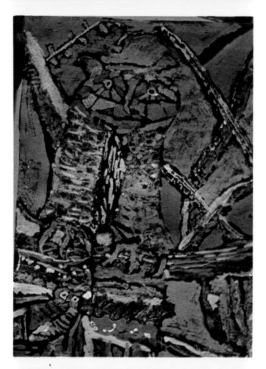

The following guidelines are recommended for the painting process: Unless the youngsters can mix subtle colors individually on a palette (pie tin or TV dinner tray), prepare in advance, with student help, enough small containers of paint (half-pint milk or juice cartons rinsed thoroughly are suggested—these can be resealed with a rubberband) in assorted colors, neutrals and tints with a watercolor brush for each. For a class of thirty students, approximately three dozen containers of assorted hues, including whites and greys, should be mixed beforehand. If the students work at tables, several containers can be placed on each table, and students can share colors or mix other colors from the hues available. The reason for pre-mixing of colors is to avoid dependence on the harsh primary colors of pure red, yellow or blue. Tints of colors, produced by adding white to the color, are quite successful in the tempera-batik process. Avoid the use of very dark colors since the final effect depends upon the color contrasting against the black ink lines.

Remind the students from time to time that *the surface left unpainted will be black in the final product*. Students should paint up to the chalk lines, leaving them unpainted. Youngsters should choose their colors carefully because *once the tempera dries on the paper, changes cannot be made*. A color painted over a dried color will wash off in the final rinsing process. For special effects, wet-on-wet color will work for texture or pattern.

98

Subject matter for tempera batiks is most exciting when there are strong possibilities to incorporate patterns, as in birds, insects, and fish. Top—Grade 7. University School, Iowa City, Iowa. Bottom—Grade 8. University School, Iowa City, Iowa.

Students should be encouraged to use more than one value of a color in the sky, in the foreground, in the feathers of a bird, in leaves on a tree. The sky area can often be varied in color through arbitrary design shapes created by tree branches, telephone poles or power lines.

When the painting is finished and completely dry, it should be coated with black India ink either undiluted or in a ratio of three parts ink to one part water. Before inking, wipe off the excess white chalk with a cloth. A two-inch utility brush is usually used to apply the ink. The teacher should demonstrate the ink application, cautioning the students to brush carefully and evenly in a horizontal direction to prevent any ink splatter on their clothes and to avoid excessive brushing which could disintegrate paint film. A table protected by newspapers should be designated as the inking table and the ink should be put in a sturdy container that will not tip over. Each student should have a protective piece of newspaper under his painting when he inks it. The ink-covered paintings should be stored to dry for several hours.

The ink removal process should be supervised by the teacher while the rest of the students are given another art assignment to keep them busy. Rinsing can be done at a sink or outdoors in good weather by using a water spray hose.

To protect the painting from tearing during the rinsing or washing, it should be placed on a piece of masonite, formica or heavy plastic the size of the painting itself or preferably slightly larger.

Top—Tempera batik. Grade 8. Iowa City, Iowa. Center— the first step in painting the tempera-India ink batik. Note the pink areas of the background construction paper which were left unpainted. Bottom—The completed batik after the ink had been applied, allowed to dry overnight, and rinsed off. Do not over-rinse.

If a spray attachment is available for the sink faucet, use it. The water may be lukewarm or cold. Run the water first over the whole painting so it adheres to the board or plastic sheet, then sponge the whole painting softly and keep rotating the painting under the water spray until the desired effect is achieved. Sometimes the ink adheres strongly to an area and must be sponged more thoroughly or rubbed off with the fingers while rinsing. The best tempera batiks are those which retain some ink as textural effects on the colored areas. There are, of course, many stages at which the rinsing can be halted. The student with the teacher's guidance will have to judge when the effect needed is achieved.

After a final rinsing to remove the excess ink-stained water, the painting should be blotted with paper towels and allowed to dry thoroughly. Batiks may be enriched, if desired, by coating them with clear shellac or liquid wax. Any retouching of the work should be checked by the teacher since excessive touching-up tends to destroy the quality of the tempera-batik technique.

This batik process can be done on unbleached muslin if a little starch is added to the tempera paint. Place newspapers under the stretched muslin when painting and, when the tempera is thoroughly dry, the cloth can be crumbled or crushed before applying the India ink. The ink will flow into the cracked lines and create a true batik effect.

100

Shops, beauty parlors, filling stations, and bridges can often become the locale for an after-school or weekend sketch that can develop into a tempera-ink batik. Ninth-grade youngsters sketched after school in a supermarket, Athens, Georgia. Opposite Page—Results of project by eighth-grade students. Iowa City, Iowa.

Monoprint negative (Grade 8). Iowa City, Iowa. The process: A brayer with oil ink was rolled over a piece of 12" × 18" window glass (its edges taped to prevent cutting), completely covering the glass. A sheet of thin paper (cream manila or thin poster) was placed over the glass. On top of this the student placed the preliminary line drawing made on newsprint. Using a small empty paper box in the left hand to anchor the paper without smudging it, the student used a pencil and retraced the line drawing with a definite pressure. The result: a monoprint. After the first print is taken with the lines in black, a second paper can be pressed over the inked glass and a negative print will result with the lines appearing light.

PRINTMAKING

Printmaking in its many varied techniques and complex aspects has a unique and constant appeal for the young adolescent.

Boys especially are challenged by the possibilities of cutting or gouging designs into the wood or linoleum blocks and by the *manly* ability needed to manipulate the heavy roller press. Both boys and girls anxiously look forward to the *moment of truth,* the pulling of their initial print.

Because of these built-in attractions, the teacher will have little trouble introducing printmaking projects into the program.

Linoleum-print projects where the subject matter is limited to non-object shapes and which require only a few random cuts with the linoleum gouge and a quick print or two are relatively easy to supervise and keep the youngsters occupied for about an hour but, unfortunately, they accomplish only superficial results. Qualitative printmaking in the junior high school is another story altogether. The best prints, whether monotype, linoleum or wood block, collograph, acetate or cardboard intaglio require special preplanning on the part of teacher and student.

Everyday places and events often present the student with the most effective subject matter for prints, as in the case of this woodblock print by a young Japanese teenager. Notice how the ordinary becomes extraordinary through the medium of the print.

103

Subject matter for a print project should not be chosen indiscriminately. For woodblocks and linocuts an effective dark and light composition with variety of shapes and contrast of pattern and texture should be the goal. Teachers have found the following motivational possibilities helpful: Visits to natural museums, photographs, films and color slides on insects, fish, spiderwebs, exotic flowers, plants, birds and wild animals. A portrait of a friend, classmate or self-portrait is well adapted to the block print technique. A cityscape with interesting detail and break-up of space is highly recommended. Industrial sites, gas stations, junk yards, antique shops, bus or train terminals, airports, still-life arrangements—all provide challenging subject matter. Generally a preliminary sketch for all print projects is recommended. The sketching instrument depends on the kind of print technique to be utilized. In block prints a blunt felt nib pen or small brush and black ink may be used, the dark areas indicated with solid ink application. In the majority of cases the contour-drawing technique is recommended for preliminary sketches because it requires the student to include those details that give vitality and complexity to the composition. It is important for the students to remember that the final print will be just the reverse of the sketch unless the drawing is transposed when it is transferred to the block.

In engravings or intaglio type prints on acetate, aluminum or glossy-surfaced cardboard, a preliminary sketch in pencil or fine pen and ink is recommended since the final product often depends on the sensitive line quality achieved.

For linoleum or woodblock prints it is recommended that the students plan their dark and light values in black ink, ink wash or pencil on a preliminary sketch so they will know what to cut out (light areas) and what to leave uncut (dark areas). Another possibility for planning the light and dark schema is to draw the preliminary sketch with white crayon on black paper. This presents the student with somewhat the same effect he achieves in the printed block. The white crayon on black and the cut of the gouge both produce light lines or areas. Sometimes it is helpful to the student if he marks a small *x* identifying those parts of the block that should be cut out.

The following suggestions have been found helpful in producing block prints:

Use blocks or plates large enough to give the student ample opportunity for a developed composition. A minimum size of 9 by 9 inches or 9 by 12 inches is recommended. Maximum size up to 18 × 24 inches.

Be certain there are enough linoleum gouges in various sizes and that these have been sharpened, if necessary.

Opposite Page, Right and Left—Two fine woodblocks (Grade 8). Oyodo Middle School, Osaka, Japan. A sensitive preliminary drawing preceded the transfer to the block before actual cutting. Center—Another sensitively-handled woodblock portrait (Grade 8). Iowa City, Iowa.

Students can be encouraged to create subtle light values in a print by cutting carefully into the block or plate, but not too deeply, so that the low relief may produce a textural effect.

Directional gouging with the tool can give unity to the design. The negative (light) areas in a direction echo the contour of the positive (dark) object next to it. The analogy here is somewhat like ripples in a stream when rain is falling—ripples forming around each drop of rain merge into ripples of adjacent raindrops. Thus unity and variety are achieved simultaneously.

The transfer of the sketch to the block can be achieved by using black carbon paper and tracing the composition. Another method is to place the sketch in pencil with all dark areas filled in face down on the linoleum or similar plate and run it through a heavy-duty press. The pressure transfers the image to the plate or block. Make a trial run to test the pressure. One merit of this method is that the sketch is then reversed on the block and, when finally printed, it will be in the same format as the original composition.

106

Top Right—Student from Oyodo Middle School, Osaka, Japan, as the model, attired in a Kendo uniform, a traditional sport popular with the young men of Japan. Top Left—A detailed contour drawing of the model. Bottom Left—Resulting woodblock print. (Grade 7.)

Some recommendations concerning the inking and printing of blocks or plates follow:

Use newsprint for trial prints. Colored tissue, brown Kraft paper, colored construction paper, tissue collage, magazine ads, rice paper, muslin cloth and bogus paper may be utilized for the final prints.

If possible designate an inking table or area, a printing area and a clean-up area. Unless there is some semblance of order during these operations in print-making, confusion can develop.

For the inking area cover a table with newspaper and on this table organize the inking slabs (these may be 12-inch squares or 12- by 18-inch rectangles of either lacquer-coated masonite, glass with edges taped, cookie sheets, or commercial ink slabs), the printing inks and the brayers or ink rollers. Do not economize on the brayers. Order the best quality because if care is taken they will outlast the cheaper variety by years.

The printing area may be either another table covered with newspapers or the student's own working desk or area which also should be protected by newspapers. To get a good print without the use of a press, the student can use as the pressure instrument the palm of his hand, a spoon, the cover of a glass jar if it has smooth rounded edges, the Japanese baren, the rounded wooden handle of a linoleum gauge, or a brayer. Many teachers claim the metal tablespoon is most effective.

Top—Collograph. James Madison Junior High, Seattle. Following a carefully planned composition, the student used glue to adhere an assortment of materials to chipboard. After linear effects were etched in, the plate was given a coat of "Rez" wood sealer, inked, and printed like regular intaglio. Right—Collograph. Japan.

107

Top Left—Using the tablespoon as a baren to take a print. Top Right — Making preliminary drawing for a monoprint. (See page 115, lower left.) Center Left—Creating a textural effect with nail holes in the wood block.

Center Right—Taking a proof print by placing very thin paper over the block, then rubbing over it with the side of a dark crayon of oil pastel. Bottom Left—Inking the plate. Bottom Right— Pulling a print. Oshkosh, Wis.

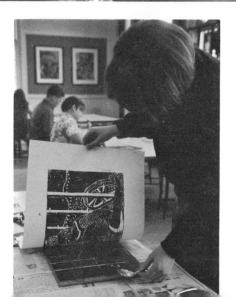

If a heavy-duty press is used, it should be mounted securely at one end of a table and tested by the teacher for correct pressure before allowing the students to operate it. Instructions in using the press should be given—where to grasp the turning handles and how to keep the rollers moving consistently. When not in use, the press should be stored so that there is no pressure on the rubber roller. This injunction also applies to ink brayers.

For linoprints and woodblocks, water-soluble printing inks may be used. These greatly reduce the problem of clean-up. However, many teachers prefer oil-base printing inks because of the quick drying factor and the ease with which they are applied to the plate. For monoprinting and engraving, however, oil-base printing ink is a necessity.

An area, a table or counter for clean-up is vitally important in printmaking, especially if the process utilizes oil-base ink. If water-soluble printing inks are used, most of the clean-up can be done at the sink.

Where oil-base printing ink is used, the cleaning area should be thoroughly covered with newspaper. Paper towels and cleaning rags should be available (students can bring discarded shirts, towels, or sheeting from home), and sufficient cleaning fluid—turpentine, kerosene or the equivalent—should be on hand. Instruct the students in the proper clean-up of their plates and the place to store them. Designate students to clean the inking slabs and brayers. Allow sufficient time for this clean-up.

Linoleum block reduction print. Grade 9, University School, Oshkosh, Wisconsin. Reduction prints achieve their special effect by repeated color over color printing of the same block as the surface is reduced through cutting. Colors are usually applied from light to dark.

109

There will always be the problem of students who have finished their prints and find time on their hands. A wise teacher will prepare for this contingency in advance by assigning a subsequent project. This could be a drawing from memory, a written evaluation of the print the student has made, a cartoon for the school paper or, if an art text is available, an assigned chapter to read.

The knowledgeable teacher knows that in projects such as linoleum and woodblock printing the students are eager to get to the printing stage as rapidly as possible, and it is here where the teacher's skill and patience are challenged. He must be able to counsel each student as he makes his preliminary value sketch and later as he cuts into the linoleum or woodblock, so that the student stays with the composition until he has achieved the project's objectives. Some students hurry to take an ink impression after only a few cuts in the plate. If the teacher allowed this practice in a large class of thirty or more students, the inking, printing and clean-up situation would become unmanageable. It is recommended that students take test prints by making a rubbing. To do this, newsprint or onion-skin paper is placed over the incised woodblock or linoleum and the side of a dark crayon or oil pastel is applied with an even pressure. The teacher should demonstrate this process of taking a proof print.

110

Unusual linoleum or cardboard prints result when the block is printed over a colored tissue pattern or over a magazine color layout. Make tissue collage by applying torn tissue from light to dark.

In these linoprints colored tissue torn or cut is applied with
clear polymer or laundry starch to white construction paper
slightly larger than the size of the print. More pressure is
needed than for an ordinary print, so bear down with tablespoon or baren. Be sure that the tissue is pasted down completely and is thoroughly dry before applying ink to plate or
block.

111

Top—Japanese youngster sketching at shipbuilding site and resulting woodblock from the project. Bottom—Glossy surface cardboard plate engraving. Approximately 12″ × 18″. (Process described on page 15.) Opposite Page—Woodblock printed with tempera in several stages. Grade 7, University School, Iowa City, Iowa.

Print made from engraving on X-ray plate. Grade 8, Iowa City, Iowa. Discarded X-ray plates can be cleaned with a bleach solution, then engraved with pins, needles, sandpaper, old dental tools, etc. Oil ink is then daubed all over them to penetrate the engraved areas; they are wiped clean with paper towels and printed on semi-moist paper. A heavy roller press must be used. Proofs may be obtained by rubbing charcoal into the engraved areas, but the plate must be cleaned with turpentine before inking. If a black sheet of construction paper is placed under the plate while engraving, the cut lines will show up more clearly. Large-sized prints should be stretched by gum-taping them to a masonite sheet to dry.

Top Left, Center, and Right—Linoleum prints over colored-tissue collage. Grade 7, University School, Oshkosh, Wisconsin. Bottom Left and Right—Monoprints in multi-colors (grades 7 and 9). The student places his preliminary drawing under glass and, using fairly thick tempera or monoprint medium, paints in the areas as he desires. Then placing his sheet of paper (this may be colored construction paper) over the coated glass, he takes his print by firmly pressing the paper down with baren, heel of hand, brayer, or tablespoon. For a final effect he may clean the glass plate, paint in the linear effects with black tempera, and placing the dried print over the glass, achieve his dark linear pattern.

Mixed media collage by ninth-grade girl, Athens, Georgia.
Project began with sketches of matadors and toreadors from
photos, and slides. After a space-filling composition was inked
in, tissue and patterned segments from a magazine were
applied. The surface was heavy white paper which permitted
overlapping of colored tissues to create new colors.

COLLAGE

The collage process and its related family of montage, mosaic, collograph and assemblage, have provided art teachers with one of the most exciting and effective avenues for introducing the young student to art structure, design, space, color, value, pattern and texture. In collage, the adolescent has the unique opportunity of rearranging and changing his placement of pictorial and design elements until he achieves a satisfying and fulfilling composition.

A preliminary drawing or sketch is generally recommended as a basic reference in the case of a collage dealing with the landscape, figure study or still-life arrangement. In themes from the imagination fantasy or purely non-objective interpretations, direct cutting, tearing and application may be encouraged but in both cases the pasting or permanent adhering of materials usually should be postponed until the youngster, with the teacher's guidance, has a chance to evaluate his work and make those compositional changes and revisions that may be needed to enhance his work.

Steps in creating a paper collage. Grade 8, University School, Oshkosh, Wisconsin. Top—The preliminary sketch. Middle— Decisions, decisions! Bottom—One of the many aesthetic interpretations. Stuart Davis would approve, we believe.

117

The collage technique has unlimited possibilities so far as subject matter and expressive materials are concerned. "Found" materials have added a whole new dimension to the collage aesthetic. Experienced teachers have discovered the following collage projects highly successful:

Colored-construction-paper collage on construction paper as a background. Black, white and gray construction paper can be effectively used with colored papers.

Wallpaper collage (old wallpaper sample books are available to teachers) in which the assorted colors, patterns and textures lend themselves to imaginative themes. Wallpaper can be combined effectively with cloth remnants. A heavier background paper should be used for wallpaper collages. Cardboard from packing cartons or grey chipboard, where budgets allow it, may be utilized.

Old magazines and periodicals have proven a proverbial gold mine for collage projects, especially in schools where the art supply is limited. Armed with glue or white paste, scissors, a sheet of colored construction paper and a few magazines, young adolescents can create exciting compositions and simultaneously learn how usually discarded materials can be transformed through artistic endeavor, where the whole creation is much more exciting and definitely greater than the sum of its parts.

Another approach to collage, Oshkosh, Wisconsin. The eighth-grade art class stained or painted all kinds of scrap paper—manila, construction, etc.—then used these in a composition suggesting the terrain or a city from the air. Note especially how they tore the paper and created the lighter rough edges that add immeasurably to the design.

Colored-tissue-paper collage has found favor with youngsters of all ages, but today it is being combined with mixed-media collage, where colored tissue is contrasted with magazines and cut-outs, with felt-pen contour drawing or with "found" materials.

If the student wants the colored-tissue collage to retain a vibrant color, or if he wants to create new, bright colors through overlapping, the basic background must be white paper, white tag or a white painted surface. Adhesives for applying the tissue have varied over the years. Originally, diluted shellac was utilized and is sometimes still used today. However, the problems of clean-up and the necessity for special dissolvents discouraged many students and teachers. Liquid white glue diluted about 50 percent with water became more popular as a tissue adhesive but students had to be careful to use permanent ink, either felt nib or pen, for their background drawings because the diluted glue dissolved the ink and bled into the tissue. Today many teachers recommend laundry starch because it works as an adhesive, is inexpensive and, with its use, work tables are easy to clean. However, the preliminary ink drawings must still be made in permanent ink if starch adhesive is used, and sometimes the color of the starch tints certain light-colored tissue papers.

Some teachers have found the wax crayon effective for the underlying linear composition in a tissue collage. The virtue of this process is that many colors can be exploited and either liquid glue or starch can be used since the crayon lines will not dissolve to stain the tissue.

Opposite Page, Top—Magazine ad collage on colored construction paper. Bottom—Cloth remnants glued to chipboard. Initial drawing with felt nib markers. This Page—Collage. "Found" papers. Grade 8, Oshkosh, Wisconsin. Overleaf—The posed model as a challenging subject for a collage. Grade 7, Clarke County Junior High School, Athens, Georgia.

119

Following are some recommended procedures for applying the tissue: Use soft bristle inch or half-inch utility brushes. Apply the adhesive (starch) to the background surface first in an area slightly larger than the piece of tissue to be adhered. Place the torn or cut piece of tissue down carefully over the moistened area and apply another coat of starch over the tissue from center outward making sure every edge is adhered securely. Occasionally wash out the brush in water since some of the tissue color pigment is picked up by the brush. If a preliminary drawing is made on the white background surface with a black crayon, permanent ink pen or marker, it is recommended that the tissue pieces applied be torn slightly larger than the drawn objects or shapes. The inked or crayoned lines will come through and unite the composition. If the lines disappear under the darker tissues, they can be inked or crayoned again if necessary when the composition is complete; or a coat of shellac, which may be applied to the finished and dried collage, will bring out the inked contour lines. It is usually a good idea to begin tissue collage with the lighter-colored tissues. Once a dark-colored tissue is applied it is difficult to change it to a lighter value with tissue alone. If such a change is really necessary, white paper (typewriter paper is suggested) must be glued over the dark tissue area before the color value can be lightened. Sometimes the application of a light tissue over a dark tissue, such as white over dark blue or pale pink over dark green, will produce a subtle, unusual, glazing effect without significantly changing the basic value.

The landscape, too, has many possibilities for a collage interpretation, especially sites where buildings are a maze of doors, windows, porches, stairways, grills, antennae, smoke stacks, and ventilators. Top and Center—Students use their sketches as reference for their collage. Bottom—Collage by adolescent attending an American school in Athens, Greece.

Mixed-media collage, grade 7, University School, Oshkosh, Wisconsin. A dark colored construction paper background helps to unify the diverse materials.

PLASTER RELIEF

Young adolescents respond with high enthusiasm to the technique of making plaster reliefs because it often involves a new approach to clay and plaster and, like the linoprint, it includes the added element of surprise when they separate the plaster cast from the clay and see the results of their efforts. Teenagers in an art room can now make larger, free-form shaped reliefs by using a piece of tempered masonite as a working surface and by building a clay wall around their slab of clay. The processes involved in making sculptural reliefs based on a clay-slab negative inside a cardboard carton are described in detail on pages 118–120 in *Emphasis: Art,* but the evaluative aspects and considerations of this technique bear repeating.

Opposite Page—Plaster reliefs, grade 7, Iowa City, Iowa. Project began with sketches at museum. Note how objects pressed in negative clay mold created subtle patterns. Notice, too, how composition of animal fills the space. Also, how metallic patina brings out highlights. This Page—Steps in making plaster relief from clay negative.

125

EVALUATING A PLASTER RELIEF

Did the student use clay of the proper consistency?

Did he make his clay slab thick enough, one-half to one inch, so that a definite relief effect producing highlights and shadows in the final product is achieved?

Did he make his clay wall high enough and secure enough?

Did he utilize an assortment of "found" objects and clay tools to create varied textures and patterns as contrasts against the plain or unembellished areas of clay?

Did he realize as he worked that the impressions he made in the clay will be reversed or in bas-relief in the final plaster product?

Did he mix the plaster of Paris and water in the correct manner and in the necessary proportions?

Did he mix sufficient plaster of Paris to fill the clay mold so that his completed relief would be at least one inch or more in thickness, thus preventing breakage?

Did he remember to put in a metal or wire hook in the moist plaster before it dried if he desired to display the work as a wall relief?

After separating the plaster from the clay mold, did he wash off the relief carefully using a stiff brush to remove the clay from the recessed areas?

Did he remember to file or sandpaper the excess or sharp edges of the dried plaster relief before adding finishing touches?

Did he give the plaster relief a coat of white glue, clear polymer or shellac if he planned to stain it?

Did he enhance the relief by staining it, using either diluted oil paints, wood stains or commercial patinas like Rub 'n' Buff or Sculpmetal?

Animals, birds, insects, and fish lend themselves effectively to plaster-relief themes. Suggest students limit the oil stain colors to neutrals at first in order to achieve variety. Be sure that plaster-relief has one or two coats of shellac or white glue before staining. Allow liquid stain to flow into incised lines. Achieve highlights by wiping raised surfaces.

THREE-DIMENSIONAL PROJECTS

There is no doubt that young adolescents, especially boys, enjoy working with materials they can carve, model or construct three-dimensionally. The major problem in such projects is not so much one of motivation as it is of procedure, special techniques, clean-up and storage. A class of thirty or more students working on additive or subtractive sculpture presents certain organizational difficulties that must be resolved.

The teacher must decide beforehand if he wants the entire class to engage in the same project or allow the students to work in a variety of materials. If he can control a large class where some youngsters are working on ceramics pots, some on plywood or balsa wood construction, some on plaster carving and others on wire sculpture, it is a tribute to his teaching skill, provided, of course, that the resulting works show evidence of the student's growth in three-dimensional design. If, as is often the case, the teacher becomes merely the dispenser of a variety of materials and tools needed by the various groups and has no time to evaluate the work-in-process with the youngsters, then it is much wiser to teach one sculptural technique with the entire class participating. In such instances, the teacher can organize materials, tools and storage space more effectively; he can plan motivational resources

Wire-and-metal sculpture has a definite appeal for adolescents. Top—Using wire as a contour line to delineate form. Center—Group project using metal "found" objects. Bottom—Space modulator in wire and metal. Students must learn to use the soldering iron for complex metal projects.

127

  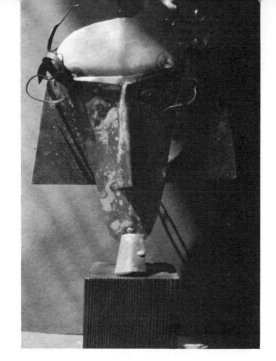

to benefit the whole class; his general evaluations will have meaning for all the students; and the youngsters themselves will learn much from each other's efforts.

The following guidelines are suggested for teaching various three-dimensional art projects:

Be certain sufficient materials and tools for the specific project are on hand before the activity begins.

Check to see that adequate storage facilities will be available for the project-in-process. If a teacher meets several classes a day in the same art room, he will have to plan carefully so that the projects for the various classes are spaced throughout the semester, quarter or school year; otherwise he will find the storage problem critical.

More time must be allotted for materials distribution and clean-up, especially when the projects involve plaster, foamglass, clay and wood scraps, paper-mâché or "found" object construction.

Some teachers have discovered that plaster block sculpture clean-up can be expedited by having students do the carving inside a shallow cardboard carton. Hopefully this keeps the excess plaster off desks and floors. In fair weather students may do their carving outside the school building, but even in these instances newspapers should be used to protect excess plaster from littering lawns or sidewalks.

If students are expected to bring their own "found" materials for a construction project, sufficient time

There is a wealth of material adolescents can use for subtractive sculpture. Left and Center—Projects in alabaster and driftwood. Right—An additive sculpture made from discarded metal sheeting and wire. Note how wooden base of pleasing proportions enhances the sculpture.

must be allowed for the material to be collected. The teacher must expect to remind students several days in advance to bring the necessary materials. A paper shopping bag labelled with the students' name can be used to store their "found" materials. In some cases where youngsters do not have the time or the opportunity to locate materials, the teacher must provide an alternate project for them.

In sculpting projects in plaster, wood, foamglass or soft firebrick, a preliminary sketch or a working model in plasticine or clay is recommended. Some teachers prefer to have the youngster work directly in the material. For non-objective, free-form themes the direct method of carving excels, but most adolescents who

wish to sculpt a figure, a head, an animal, bird or fish prefer to start with a sketch of some sort to guide them.

In all three-dimensional projects the students should be encouraged to evaluate their work-in-process from all sides and all angles, to consider variety of forms, utilization of space, relationship of elements, rhythmic movement, emphasis, and affinitive and honest use of materials.

In subtractive sculpture, students should be cautioned not to carve out or delineate one specific area at a time but gradually to achieve a unified form by rotating their sculpture as they cut away.

When sculpting animals, heads or human figures, youngsters should be guided to keep the base undefined

More examples of subtractive sculpture by young adolescents. Left—Driftwood. Center—Pumice stone. Also commercially available as Featherstone. Right—A carving from a plaster of Paris mold with a slight additive of fine-grain zonolite.

during most of the carving process so the piece does not become top-heavy and fall over and break, unless, of course, the student plans a supplementary support of metal rod or dowel set in a wood base.

Appendages such as legs, arms, ears, horns, beaks, fins, tails and jutting accessories should be kept undefined until the basic shape is well established. Once the material is carved away it is difficult and sometimes impossible to make corrections.

The carved sculpture, whether in soft firebrick, plaster, Sculpstone, Featherock, foamglass or wax, should be conceived to ensure the greatest utilization of the block. Students should be cautioned against subject matter themes or motifs that are too intricate and that might be more easily achieved in wood, clay, wire or metal.

Textural or decorative details on a carving should be delineated during the last stages, but students should be reminded that no amount of texture or pattern will redeem or enhance the piece if the basic, unembellished form is weak. This means that the student together with the teacher's help must evaluate his work in its early stages, much in the same way that a preliminary sketch for a painting is critically appraised.

The principle of emphasis utilized expressively can often give vitality to a sculptural form. Students should be guided to see the heightened aesthetic possibilities in the delineation of characteristic features: the claws or beak of an eagle, the horns of a bull or ram, the eyes of an owl, the mane of a horse, or the teeth of a jaguar.

Top—A sensitively rendered relief on black slate by a youngster from England. Middle—Reed, discarded fur, and beads make up this very personal insect. Grade 7, Iowa City, Iowa. Bottom—Foamglass, available in blocks, is the medium used for this fish form. The material has an unpleasant odor when carved. Ventilate art room or do the carving outdoors.

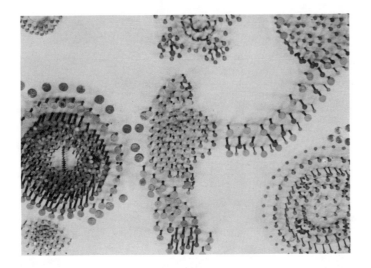

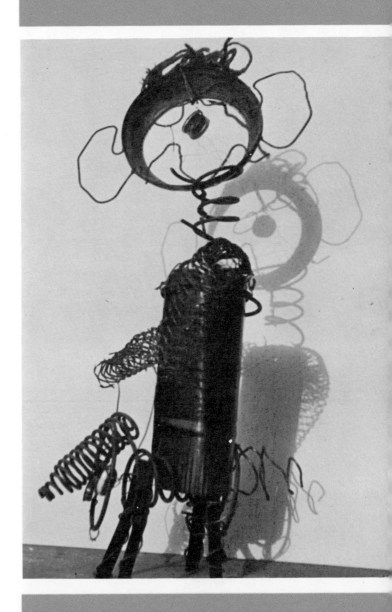

A complementary base for the completed carved sculpture is generally recommended. Driftwood, discarded blocks of wood from a lumber yard or from a dismantled building, and sections of tree trunks with the bark remaining often give stature and distinction to the finished work. The blocks of wood can be stained or painted to contrast with the sculpture.

For more technical information on sculpture projects including masks, stabiles, reliefs, paper box construction and plaster mold carving which may be adapted for the junior high school art program, see *Emphasis: Art.*

Top—Construction with assorted nails, grade 8, England. Right—In this day of junk assemblage, it is interesting to note that this very "in" horse and rider was created by an adolescent art student two decades ago. Washington, Iowa Public Schools. Following two pages show examples of subtractive sculpture in plaster of Paris and firebrick.

131

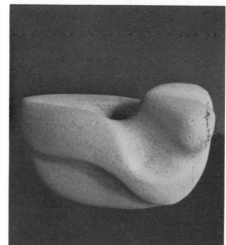

APPROACHES TO CERAMICS

Generally teachers recommend one or two class sessions of exploration with clay media before tackling a specific ceramic project, but the initial experimental activity must not be allowed to degenerate into purposeless handling of the material. Students should be guided to discover what clay is and what it can do: to pull, press, roll, pinch and mold the clay, to discover textures by using assorted tools and their fingers, to build form-on-form or form-within-form, to combine pinch pots, slabs, coils and pellets of clay into organized structures.

A very important consideration in every clay project is that the prepared clay be of the correct plasticity or consistency, neither too moist nor too dry, or it may cause frustrating problems for teacher and students. The instructor should check out the condition of the clay at least a day or two before the project begins.

If the students are given a ball of clay about the size of a large grapefruit and then instructed to hold it in their hands as they manipulate or form it, the teacher will divert the tendency of some youngsters to treat the clay two-dimensionally. This approach is especially effective when the subject matter or motif is birds, fish or animals. Once the student has achieved the characteristic sculptural form of the animal, he can add appendages and details in the usual manner, turning the clay piece as he works.

For some youngsters there is no greater fascination than building forms out of clay as this illustration of a seventh-grade boy, intent on his creation, attests. Experiences in ceramics should be a part of every exemplary art program.

Another recommended and successful technique in clay construction, especially when making animals, is the *post and lintel* approach described in detail in *Emphasis: Art*. The adolescent should be guided to achieve the special characteristics of the animal he is creating: the sway or turn of the body, the stance or counterstance of the legs, the swing of the tail, the bend of the head, the flow of the mane.

The sky is the limit when it comes to textural exploitation of the clay form. "Found" objects such as bottle caps, nails, screws, nuts and bolts, wire screening, cord, clothespins, broken bandsaw blades, combs, sea shells, old keys, beads, buttons, coins, checkers, wire lathing, steel wool, and drinking straws—all provide their special and unique textures or patterns in clay.

In the overcrowded junior high school classes of today, the teacher would find it difficult if not impossible to instruct every youngster in the sophisticated, highly technical and time-consuming craft of throwing pottery on a wheel. Rather than frustrate a majority of students by demanding skills that college ceramics majors, craftsmen and an occasional senior high school student work long hours to possess, the teacher might concentrate on programming handbuilt techniques which the young teen group can master.

These highly sophisticated branch pots (approximately 12″ high), by seventh-grade students in the University School, Oshkosh, Wisconsin, began with the pinch pot method illustrated on page 139. Note the variety of shapes achieved, the complementary textures and patterns that embellish the vessels, and the subtle application of stain and patina.

135

Once the problems of clay supply, preparation, storage of work-in-process and supplementary tools and materials are identified and resolved, the teacher must consider the important aspects of student motivation and stimulation. The youngsters must be challenged to avoid the trite, tasteless and poorly designed bud vases, ashtrays and insipid figurines, and to aim instead for honest, personal, individual, earthy, and organic forms. The instructor should guide the students to seek inspiration in the natural world for limitless sources of three-dimensional design.

Encourage them to collect an assortment of stones, pebbles, seedpods, shells, nuts and pieces of driftwood and to share these discoveries with their classmates. Plan an exhibit of the collected items where the youngsters can examine them at leisure. Enrich their backgrounds by showing selected close-up photographs of natural forms, and color slides and films that emphasize the variety of design in nature. Ask them to experiment with the clay, to try to capture the quality of texture in the rough bark of a tree, the striations of an eroded rock, the intricacies of a honeycomb, or the modulation of a sea shell. Challenge them to discover new textures with an assortment of tools or "found" objects. Alert them to the almost endless variety of forms in pods, pebbles and nuts that could serve as the catalyst for their own clay containers or constructions.

Other recommended motivations might include a demonstration of pottery techniques by the teacher or visiting craftsman; a bulletin board exhibit of ceramic work by Peter Voulkos, Harvey Littleton, Shoji

More of the distinctive microphotography of nature's wonders by Dr. W. Robert Nix. What inspiration these would be for projects in ceramic structure and decoration!

Hamada, Betty Feves, Angelo Garzio, William Daley, Kenneth M. Green, Win Ng, Paul Soldner and other distinguished contemporary potters; a display of quality ceramic pieces from the teacher's collection or on loan from a local museum or art gallery; and films that deal with contemporary ceramic construction, especially slab, pinch pot and other creative handbuilt techniques.

Evaluation and critiques of clay projects-in-process should take place each period. Students should have the opportunity to appraise their efforts with the sympathetic guidance of the teacher and also to share their discoveries with classmates.

The *basic shape* in any ceramic undertaking must be the first critical concern. Whether organic, geometric, symmetric or asymmetric, it must stand by itself as an aesthetic entity, a sculptural statement. No amount of embellishment or decoration can redeem it if it is weak in concept, weak in design. At this stage the student should examine his ceramic piece from many angles.

Variety in the basic form should be a vital consideration in the total design. Because most students have been exposed to commercially made ceramics where the accent is on symmetrical styling, the teacher must be able to guide the youngsters to see the honesty or aesthetic of asymmetric delineation. Variety can also be achieved through the contrasting shapes of the appendages, of spouts, necks, feet, and bases, and through the exploitation of positive and negative spaces created by openings in the vessel, by the handles or lids, and

Top—Pinch pot branch container. Earth stains. Middle—Ceramic animal with "found" object decoration. Bottom—Large ceramic vessel has additive slab pieces as decoration. It is important to use slip when adhering slabs, pellets, or ribbons of clay to the main structure.

137

by the delineation of incised or bas-relief features to create dark and light pattern.

Unity is also vital to the aesthetic impact of clay sculpture or construction. There should be a natural flow or movement from one part to another, from one plane or contour to another. Appendages should grow naturally from the basic structure, should complement and not detract from it and should be in scale with it. This holds true for the decoration whether incised or bas-relief. It should, like the final coloring or staining, enhance the sculpture or container, not camouflage or compete with it.

Suggested Procedures in Slab Construction. At least one slab of clay for each student in class should be prepared by the teacher with student assistance in advance. Slabs should be at least one-half inch thick. A rolling pin, a burlap- or cloth-covered board, guiding strips of wood one-half inch thick, and plastic cloth (visqueen) to keep slabs moist during storage will be needed. Additional slabs can be made during the project when necessary.

"Found" objects to create textures and additional clay coils, ribbons, and pellets may be impressed on or into the moist rolled-out slab to enrich the surface. If the slab is large enough, it can be cut into smaller slabs and assembled into a sculptural form or container. With a paddle made from scrap wood approximately 1 by 2 inches thick by 18 inches long, wrapped at one end with string or cord, tap the completed construction at the joints to strengthen it. Some teachers suggest moistening the junctures where two slabs are joined with water or slip. When joints are secure, more paddling may be done to alter the shape of the sculpture to a form desired. Simultaneously the string-wrapped paddle will add a characteristic texture to the piece. Two or more slab constructions in different sizes or volumes may be joined together for a more complex sculpture.

Suggested Procedure for Pinch Pot Sculpture. For pinch pot sculpture, five pounds of moist clay per student is recommended. The clay is shaped into a ball and cut in half. The student manipulates each half into a pinch pot shape, keeping the walls fairly thick and each pot similar in size. He joins the two pinch pots together, pinching the seams tightly to form a hollow ball.

Holding the ball of clay in one hand, the student paddles it with the string-covered board described above in slab construction until the pinched seams disappear. The youngster then keeps turning the ball as he paddles. This action packs the clay and seals in enough air to support the walls. It is important that the entire clay ball is paddled evenly as it is turned. In the paddling process the student can change the shape of the ball to another organic form inspired by the contours he sees in stones, pebbles, pods or shells.

Decoration and textural details may be added in a number of ways, using "found" objects and clay tools for incising and imprinting. Relief effects may be achieved by applying pellets, thin coils, and assorted shapes or ribbons of clay. Be sure the clay is moist for this process. If not, moisten or use slip.

Opposite Page—Steps in making the basic unit for pots illustrated. Shape clay into ball and cut in half. Manipulate each half into a pinch pot, keeping walls thick and pots similar in size. Join pots together, pinching seams lightly. Tap with string-covered paddle to desired shape. Combine two or three units if desired.

Necks, feet, handles, spouts, bases and other appendages may be added for functional purposes or to enrich the form, but the sealed balls should not be opened until the whole sculpture is complete. Many exciting developments take place and discoveries made when the youngsters try to combine one or more pinch pot process balls in various sizes into one unified sculptural form.

Experienced teachers soon learn that "un"happy *accidents* can occur during the bisque firing if the clay still retains air bubbles. Proper wedging of clay will help. Adding sufficient grog to the clay will eliminate some explosion hazards. Cumbersome and heavy pieces, especially certain bulky animals, fish, and reclining figures, should be hollowed-out when leather hard. Another suggestion for the slab and pinch pot sculptures described above is to inject pin holes in them in their leather-hard stage so the air can escape during the firing.

Suggestions for Staining. For schools with relatively small art classes and adequate ceramic facilities, especially large-sized kilns, the technique of glazing can carry the ceramic process to a rich aesthetic culmination for the young adolescent. In most middle or junior high schools, however, the burgeoning sizes of classes and the limited ceramic equipment make glazing possibilities a real problem. It is relatively easy, most art teachers find, to fire greenware because raw clay products may be stacked inside or on top of one another or rest against each other in the kiln and the firing of one class's ceramic output can be accomplished in a few firings. Even engobe decoration, where the clay slip is applied to the greenware and sometimes scratched through for graffito designs, will not complicate the firing problem too much. The teacher must caution the students not to let the clay body get too dry before applying slip or *peeling* will result in the firing. *Peeling* refers to the separation of the clay body and the slip.

Glaze firing, however, is another problem altogether. The glazed bisque ware must be stacked carefully. No glazed piece may touch another piece or the wall of the firing chamber. In many cases special supports such as stilts and pins must be utilized and, if the complex stacking process is done properly, it may take weeks of glaze firing schedules, especially if the students have been challenged to create expressive clay structures of some magnitude and individuality.

Inventive teachers have discovered there are other avenues or directions in the enrichment of bisque ware. Staining is definitely one possibility. Oil and polymer stains, wood stains, waxes, enamels and oil pastels all have their unique potential in adding to the aesthetic of the bisque clay products, at the same time eliminating the long hours and weeks of supervising kiln firing. Although glazing purists sometimes question the staining approach, it is a fact that in most instances the ceramic pieces the young adolescents produce are essentially sculptural, having a fine arts emphasis rather than a utilitarian one.

Opposite Page, Center—Youngster applying color stains to completed pot. Stains can be toned down with sand or earth, or given a soft sheen with wax. Parts can be decorated using a sgraffito design. There are countless possibilities, but in the final resolution the decoration should enhance rather than disguise or destroy the fundamental form.

The various stains, especially the mineral spirit or turpentine-diluted oils in ochre, burnt or raw umber and sienna, yellow oxide, earth green and related neutral hues can be applied to the bisque ware with a cloth or one-inch utility brush, beginning with the lighter colors and making sure the stain penetrates the incised or recessed areas in the clay. Before the applied stain dries, the relief or raised surfaces should be toned down partially with a turpentine-moistened cloth so that the darker textured or patterned recessed areas will create a rich contrasting effect.

Sometimes moist dirt or soil of another shade or value than the bisque ware can be rubbed on and into the impressed or incised areas of the clay. Oil pastels, Rub 'n' Buff and other commercial patinas may be blended into the ware for rich and unusual patterns of surface color.

In almost all cases where staining and coloring is applied to clay bisque ware, it is advisable to add a protective coating to the piece. To achieve a subtle sheen rather than a hard gloss, liquid floor wax is recommended as a final coat. Sometimes several applications of the wax may be necessary. Clear polymer is also suggested as another possibility.

The utilization of opaque oils, acrylics and enamels on bisque ware must be sensitively and carefully handled. In all instances, the color decoration should add to, not detract from, the ceramic work.

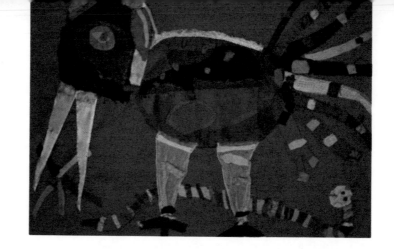

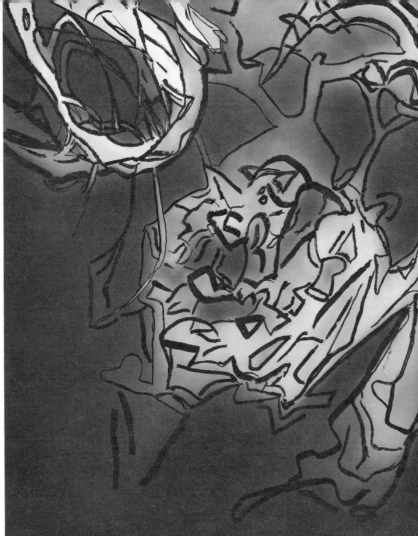

Above—High contrast photography by ninth-grade art class, Clarke County Junior High School, Athens, Georgia. Opposite Page, Top Left, and Center Left—Grade 8, University School, Oshkosh, Wisconsin. Mask construction with corrugated cardboard and diluted Sculpmetal. The Sculpmetal is given a coat of India ink and, when dry, burnished with steel wool.

Bottom Left—Grade 7, Clarke County Junior High School, Athens, Georgia. Papier-mâché masks painted with brilliant polymer acrylics. Top Right—Fabric appliqué. West Berlin middle school. Center Right—Japanese youngsters engaged in a poster design project. Bottom Right—Intricate pen-and-ink design. Newton, Mass. Junior High School.

9

THE ART ROOM

One of the art teacher's chief assets is his opportunity to make the art room a significant influence in the lives of his students, indeed, in the lives of all visitors to the room. The art room should be more than just another classroom. It should be visually inviting, colorfully keyed, its interest quotient kept high by a changing display of art, either by original work of students and professional artists, by exhibits of crafts both ancient and contemporary, or by reproductions of great art of the past. The conviction, taste and character of the art teacher are reflected in the art room. The room mirrors the vitality and calibre of the art program currently in action.

Cleanliness and order, too, have a place in the junior high school art room. A room where dirt and dust have been allowed to settle for years on plaster reproductions or on the frames of ancient sepia prints, where bulletin displays are withering with age, where storage cabinets and drawers are cluttered with unused faded papers and dried paints, and where table tops are crusted with layers of tempera, is not an example of *art in action,* nor is it an inspiration to the students.

In a sense the art room can be compared to the kitchen of a home which can be drab, sterile and negatively antiseptic or, conversely, attractive, cheerful and colorful, depending on the housekeeper whose personality it usually reflects. Some educators insist that the art room is a continuing work center and that disorder and clutter are justified at all times. Practicality demands another interpretation and here again the kitchen analogy is suggested. When the preparation of a meal is in process, it is necessary that all tools, all ingredients, be in use and in sight. When the meal is over and the utensils are washed, the kitchen is put in order for the facilitation of another preparation. The utilization of the art room should be conducted along the same lines.

During the laboratory or studio period the visitor to the art class might well feel he has stepped into a bedlam of colorful chaos, but at the end of the class period work-in-process, the cleaned tools and excess materials should be stored in their proper places and the room readied for another class and another project. Valuable time is consumed, it is true, when clean-up

---

Opposite Page—Students assembling art exhibit in school gym. Commercial panels, such as these, can be set up in school hallways or even in art rooms for additional display space. Photo courtesy of Walker Display Systems.

and storing procedures are properly and effectively carried out, but equal time is gained when incoming students do not have to waste precious minutes searching for materials and cleaning off tables for a working space. It is also a good practice for students to learn craftsmanlike procedures in studio care.

The importance of a well-appointed, well-equipped art room cannot be overemphasized in the implementation of a qualitative program. The basic requirements for such a room are specified in a number of recent professional publications. See Appendix B on recommended professional publications.

The following recommendations have been found to be especially helpful in the effective functioning of the art room:

An adequate depository facility for students' books and personal belongings near the door will alleviate the problem of cluttered drawing desks and work tables, unless, of course, such a storage space is already provided under each student's chair or drawing table.

A teacher's area equipped with coat closet, desk, filing cabinet, storage cabinets for large reproductions and color slides, cases for books and current periodicals should be strategically separated from the rest of the room by a divider or see-through screen.

Sufficient storage slots for flat work-in-process is especially important where one class follows another in quick succession. Excellent roll-away flat storage facilities for prints and paintings in process are now offered by several art supply firms.

Adequate storage space should be made for the variety of three-dimensional projects planned.

Easily constructed, inexpensive room dividers changed an uninviting, drab classroom into an efficient school art studio boasting a teacher's planning area, a crafts facility, and a general drawing and lecture area.

146

Room-darkening blinds such as black window shades or ordinary shades painted with black latex paint should be utilized.

A lectern with shelves for storage of lecture and demonstration materials is suggested for large classes.

In older school buildings where art is being offered for the first time, classrooms are often converted into art rooms. In such instances and in cases of ancient and drab art rooms, the following renovating suggestions are offered:

Paint the darkened walls, ceiling and woodwork in a light color. Non-glare paint should be used on walls and ceiling; semi-gloss enamel can be used on the woodwork. Wash all woodwork first with a strong detergent or soil remover before applying paint.

Use accents of bright color to relieve the monotony.

Stained cork bulletin boards can be painted black, dark grey or some other neutral color that will not clash with displayed art work. Clean old cork boards wth turpentine or kerosene first, and then use an oil base paint that will penetrate the cork. Latex paint can also be used. Install neutral colored vinyl floor covering.

Acoustic tile in random punch type can be glued to ceilings to counteract noise. It can also be applied to wall areas for additional bulletin or display space. For proper application, use tile adhesive. Use a retaining device on walls so that applied tiles do not shift before adhesive dries.

Equip room with modern fluorescent lighting facilities if light fixtures are inadequate.

In a large room, install movable dividers to create functional work areas. Low cost dividers can be constructed of 2- by 2-inch lumber frames and 4- by 8-feet panels of Upson or Beaverboard $\frac{1}{4}$ or $\frac{3}{8}$ inch thick. These provide excellent additional display space.

It is wise to get permission from the principal or superintendent before making renovations or alterations, but positive action usually depends on how much the art teacher believes in, and fights for, the necessary changes.

For catalogs on art room plans and furnishings write to the following firms:

Hamilton Mfg. Company, Two Rivers, Wis. 54241.
E. H. Sheldon and Company, Muskegon, Michigan.
Brunswick-Balke-Collender Co., 623 South Wabash Ave., Chicago, Ill.

For information on portable panels for displays and exhibits write to the following firms:

Sho-Walls, Brewster Corporation, Old Saybrook, Conn. 06475.
Walker Display Divider System, 520 South 21st Avenue East, Duluth, Minnesota 55812.
Porta Panel, 466 Central, Northfield, Ill. 60093.

For information on color slide storage facilities write:

Multiplex Display Fixture Co., Warne and Carter Aves., St. Louis, Mo. 63107.

YOUNG ADOLESCENTS: BEHAVIOR CLUES

They are self-conscious concerning their changing physical characteristics.

They want to be accepted by the group. Acceptance by their peers is often more important to them than approval of parent or teacher.

They may go to extremes in feelings and actions.

They develop "crushes" on the teacher.

They are often more inclined to daydream, to watch rather than to perform.

They begin to place a new emphasis on appearance, grooming and popularity.

They possess varying degrees of physiological and sexual maturity. Girls develop interest in boys sooner than boys do in girls.

They are full of physical and creative energy and can exhaust a teacher unless he paces his responses to their demands.

They are in constant communication with their friends on the major topics of dates, parties, TV, movies, sports, songs, singing groups and other boys and girls.

Many of them achieve partial economic independence through part time jobs.

Emotional instability and personality disturbances are often the rule rather than the exception at this age.

They tend to like a subject taught by a particularly likeable teacher.

Sometimes the teacher is often the only adult the adolescent has confidence in.

They are easily discouraged in their efforts, although they will try anything once. They need praise, encouragement and guidance.

They are often unusually sensitive to other people's problems and emotions. They are trying to develop a sense of values.

They do not want excessive praise in front of others, unless the activity is important in the eyes of their peers.

They have a growing desire for thrilling and new experiences.

They are in a stage of excessive hero worship. Girls usually want to be beautiful and attractive; boys want to be physically brave and to excel in sports.

They are now more and more self-critical and at the same time critical of all types of authority.

They form status groups or cliques into accepted, tolerated or rejected categories.

They fluctuate between childhood and adulthood in their interests and insights, but the main concern of most adolescents is to stop being an adolescent.

Opposite Page—Sensitive photograph by ninth-grade student, Clarke County Junior High School, Athens, Georgia. Today's revolutionary photographic and film-making techniques should certainly be part of the young adolescent's art experiences where the budget permits.

B

SUPPLEMENTAL VISUAL RESOURCES

BOOKS

Fine Arts Books for Young People, Lerner Publications Company, 133 First Avenue North, Minneapolis, Minn. 55401.

Circuses and Fairs in Art	*The Horse in Art*
Farms and Farmers in Art	*The Self-Portrait in Art*
Kings and Queens in Art	*The Ship and Sea in Art*
The Bird in Art	*The Warrior in Art*
The City in Art	

Discovering Art, 10 Volume Series, McGraw-Hill Junior Books, 330 West 42nd Street, New York, N.Y. 10036.

Time-Life Books on Artists, Time and Life Building, Chicago, Ill. 60611.

The World of Cézanne	*The World of Michelangelo*
The World of Goya	*The World of Picasso*
The World of Leonardo	*The World of Rembrandt*
The World of Manet	*The World of Rubens*
The World of Matisse	*The World of Titian*
The World of Winslow Homer	

PORTFOLIOS

Museum of Modern Art, teaching portfolios

Portfolio 1. *Modern Sculpture*
2. *Texture and Pattern*
3. *Modern Art: Old and New*
4. *Elements of Design*

Reinhold Visuals, each portfolio contains twenty-four 18- by 24-inch posters—12 in color and 12 in gravure, teachers manual. Reinhold Book Corporation, New York: Subsidiary of Chapman-Reinhold, Inc.

1. *Line*	5. *Color*
2. *Mass*	6. *Movement*
3. *Organization*	7. *Perception*
4. *Surface*	8. *Space*

Young Sculptor's Portfolio
Young Printmaker's Portfolio
Edited by F. Louis Hoover, Worcester, Mass.: Davis Publications, Inc.

Opposite Page—Japanese youngsters learn to use a brush to sketch and to create subtle colors in the early years of school. This sensitive painting by a twelve-year-old is the fruit of an in-depth art program where youngsters have time to be aware, to respond, to develop art skills, and to follow a project through to its rewarding culmination.

PICTURE STUDY PRINTS

Picture Study Prints in Color, 18 by 13 inches. Society for Visual Education, Inc., 1345 Diversey Parkway, Chicago, Ill.

1. *Common Birds*
2. *Common Insects*
3. *Spring Wild Flowers*
4. *Wild Animals*

BOOKBOX STUDY UNITS

Artist Junior Fine Arts Publications, 1346 Chapel Street, New Haven, Connecticut 06511.

I   Principles of Art
II Modern Art
III American Art
IV Great Art Movements
V Young Artists

SCULPTURAL CASTS AND REPRODUCTIONS

Alva Museum Replicas, Inc., 30-30 Norther Blvd., Long Island City, N.Y. 11101.
Austin Productions, Inc., 1615 62nd St., Brooklyn, N.Y. 11204.
Metropolitan Museum of Art, 5th Ave. at 82nd Street, New York, N.Y.
Museum Pieces, 15 Qwar 27th St., New York, N.Y. 10001.
National Gallery, Washington, D.C.
Sculpture Under the Sky, 586 Fifth Ave., New York 36, N.Y.

University Museum, University of Pennsylvania, 33rd St. and Spruce, Philadelphia, Penna.

SOURCES OF FINE ART REPRODUCTIONS AND COLOR SLIDES

Art Education, Inc., Blauvelt, N.Y. 10913.
American Library Color Slide Co., Inc., 222 West 23rd St., New York, N.Y.
Artext Prints, Inc., Westport, Connecticut.
Artist Jr., 1346 Chapel Street, New Haven, Conn. 06511.
Brentano's, 586 Fifth Avenue, New York City 10036.
Dr. Konrad Prothman, 7 Soper Avenue, Baldwin, L.I., N.Y.
Museum of Modern Art Library, 11 West 53rd Street, New York, N.Y.
National Gallery, Washington, D.C.
Metropolitan Museum of Art, Fifth Avenue and 82nd Street, New York, N.Y.
Oestreichers, 1208 6th Avenue, New York, N.Y.
Philadelphia Museum of Art, Division of Education, Parkway at 26th, Philadelphia, Pa.
Sandak, Inc., 39 West 53rd St., New York, N.Y.
School of the Art Institute of Chicago, Chicago, Ill.
Shorewood Publishers, Inc., 724 Fifth Avenue, New York, N.Y. 10019.
University Museum, University of Pennsylvania, 33rd and Spruce, Philadelphia, Pa.
University Prints, 15 Brattle Street, Harvard Square, Cambridge, Mass.
Universal Color Slide Co., 132 West 32nd St., New York, N.Y. 10001.

Periodicals the art teacher should become familiar with. Check library for availability and current addresses of publishers.

American Artist
Art Education (Journal of NAEA)
Artform
Artist Junior (for the student)
Art News
Arts and Activities
Art in Action
Ceramics Monthly
Crafts Horizons
Creative Crafts
Design Quarterly
Everyday Art (A quarterly available free of charge to art teachers from American Crayon Company, P.O. 147, Jersey City, N.J. 07303.)
Interiors
Realites
School Arts
Studies in Art Education (NAEA)
Studio International

Other magazines the teacher will find especially beneficial in certain collage and mixed-media projects.

Eye	*Look*
Harper's Bazaar	*National Geographic*
Holiday	*Seventeen*
House Beautiful	*Sports Illustrated*
House and Garden	*Vogue*
Life	*McCall's*

Top—One section of an annual state junior and senior high school exhibit sponsored by a state university, where students and teachers come to share ideas and hear nationally known artists speak. Bottom—Students viewing art reproductions. Photo courtesy of Shorewood Publishers, Inc.

BOOKS ON ADOLESCENT BEHAVIOR

The Adolescent in Your Family. Children's Bureau Publication #347. Washington, D.C.: U.S. Department of Health, Education and Welfare, 1954.

Baruch, Dorothy W. *How to Live with Your Teen-ager.* New York: McGraw-Hill, 1953.

Coleman, James S. *The Adolescent Society.* Glencoe, Ill.: Free Press, 1961.

Frank, Lawrence K., and Mary Frank. *Your Adolescent at Home and in School.* New York: Viking Press, 1956.

Garrison, Karl C. *Psychology of Adolescence,* 6th ed. Englewood Cliffs, New Jersey: Prentice-Hall, Inc., 1965.

Gesell, Arnold, Frances L. Ilg, and Louise Bates Amos. *Youth: The Years from Ten to Sixteen.* New York: Harper and Bros., 1956.

Gruhn, William T., and Karl R. Douglass. *The Modern Junior High School.* New York: Ronald Press, 1947.

Landis, Paul H. *Adolescence and Youth.* New York: McGraw-Hill, 1952.

Sebald, Hans. *Adolescence: A Sociological Analysis.* Des Moines, Iowa: Meredith Press, 1968.

Sherif, M., and C. Sherif. *Problems of Youth: Transition to Adulthood in a Changing World.* Chicago: Aldine Publishing Co., 1965.

BOOKS ON TEACHING STRATEGIES

Anderson, Donald M. *Elements of Design.* New York: Holt, Rinehart and Winston, 1961.

Burkhart, Robert C. *Spontaneous and Deliberate Ways of Learning.* Scranton, Pennsylvania: International Textbook, 1962.

De Francesco, Italo L. *Art Education: Its Means and Ends.* New York: Harper and Bros., 1958.

Fearing, Kelly, Clyde I. Martin, and Evelyn Beard. *Our Expanding Vision.* Austin, Texas: W. S. Benson Co., 1960. Books 7 and 8.

Gaitskell, Charles D., and Margaret R. Gaitskell. *Art Education During Adolescence.* New York: Harcourt, Brace and Co., 1954. Chapter III on teaching methods is as valid for teachers today as it was a decade and a half ago.

Gettings, Fred. *You Are an Artist.* London: Paul Hamlyn Ltd., 1965. The title may be misleading, but this book will have rewards and visual surprises for every junior high school art teacher.

Henkes, Robert. *Orientation to Drawing and Painting.* Scranton, Pennsylvania: International Textbook Co., 1965.

Horn, George F. *Art for Today's Schools.* Worcester, Mass.: Davis Publications, Inc., 1967. Excellent visuals by professional artists and senior high school art students, good coverage of techniques which can be adapted to the junior high school level.

————. *Bulletin Boards.* New York: Reinhold Publishing Corp., 1962.

————. *How to Prepare Visual Materials for School Use.* Worcester, Mass.: Davis Publications, Inc., 1963.

Hubbard, Guy. *Art in the High School.* Belmont, California: Wadsworth Publishing Company, Inc., 1967. Chapter 8 on Materials Resources in the Teaching of Art has a wealth of material that will be helpful to the teacher in a special art room or art studio situation.

Keiler, Manfred L. *The Art in Teaching Art.* Lincoln, Nebraska: University of Nebraska Press, 1961. A text that emphasizes the aesthetically significant role of art education in the secondary school. Should be on every school art teacher's book shelf.

La Mancusa, Katherine. *A Source Book for Art Teachers.* Scranton, Pennsylvania: International Textbook Co., 1965.

Lanier, Vincent. *Teaching Secondary Art.* Scranton, Pennsylvania: International Textbook Co., 1964.

Linderman, Earl W. *Invitation to Vision, Ideas and Imaginations for Art.* Dubuque, Iowa: Wm. C. Brown Company Publishers, 1967.

Lowenfeld, Viktor, and W. Lambert Brittain. *Creative and Mental Growth,* 4th ed. New York: Macmillan Company, 1964.

Mickish, Verle. *Creative Art: A Guide for Instructors of Junior High Grades.* Boulder, Colorado: Pruett Press, 1962.

Morman, Jean Mary. *Art: Of Wonder and a World.* Blauvelt, N.Y.: Art Education, Inc., 1967. Has strong possibilities as an appreciation of art text to supplement studio activities.

Ocvirk, Bone, and Wigg, Stinson. *Art Fundamentals, Theory and Practice,* rev. 1969. Dubuque, Iowa: Wm. C. Brown Co., 1969.

Rannells, Edward Warder. *Art Education in the Junior High School.* University of Kentucky Bureau of School Service, Bulletin #4, Vol. XVIII (1946). A classic in its field. Should be read by every junior high school art teacher.

Reed, Carl. *Early Adolescent Art Education.* Peoria, Illinois: Charles A. Bennett Co., 1957.

Richardson, Elwyn S. *In the Early World.* Wellington, New Zealand: New Zealand Council of Educational Research, 1964. A description of a dynamic art program with young adolescents in a New Zealand country school.

Shreivogel, Paul A. *The World of Art—the World of Youth.* Minneapolis, Minn.: Augsburg Publishing House, 1968.

Thompson, Beatrice. *Drawings by High School Students.* New York: Reinhold Publishing Corporation, 1966. The introduction is without doubt the most realistic description of a master art teacher's approach in a senior high school situation.

Wachowiak, Frank, and Theodore Ramsay. *Emphasis: Art.* Scranton, Pennsylvania: International Textbook Co., 1965.

BOOKS ON TECHNIQUES

Albert, Calvin, and Dorothy Seckler. *Figure Drawing Comes to Life.* New York: Reinhold Publishing Corp., 1962.

Andrews, Michael. *Creative Printmaking: For School and Camp Programs.* Englewood Cliffs, New Jersey: Prentice-Hall, Inc., 1964.

Argiro, Larry. *Mosaic Art Today,* rev. ed. Scranton, Pennsylvania: International Textbook Co., 1968.

Ball, F. Carlton, and Janice Lovoos. *Making Pottery Without a Wheel.* New York: Reinhold Publishing Corp., 1965.

Beitler, Ethel Jane. *Create with Yarn.* Scranton, Pennsylvania: International Textbook Company, 1964.

Blumenau, Lili. *Creative Design in Wall Hanging.* New York: Crown Publishers, Inc., 1968.

Brommer, Gerald F. *Wire Sculpture and Other Three-Dimensional Construction.* Worcester, Mass.: Davis Publications, Inc., 1968. An excellent and comprehensive guide to additive sculpture. Every junior high school art teacher should have this as a ready reference. Highly recommended.

Cataldo, John W. *Graphic Design.* Scranton, Pennsylvania: International Textbook Company, 1963.

————. *Lettering: A Guide for Teachers.* Worcester, Mass.: Davis Publications, Inc., 1958.

Cataldo, John W. *Words and Calligraphy for Children*. New York: Reinhold Book Corp., 1969.

Cooke, Robert W. *Designing with Light on Paper and Film*. Worcester, Mass.: Davis Publications, Inc., 1969.

Crawford, John. *Introducing Jewelry Making*. Cincinnati, Ohio: Watson Guptill Publications, 1968.

Dobkin, Alexander. *Principles of Figure Drawing*. Cleveland, Ohio: World Publishing Co., 1948.

Dommelen, David B. *Decorative Wall Hangings*. New York: Funk and Wagnall, Inc., 1962.

Erickson, Janet Doub, and Adelaide Sproul. *Printmaking Without a Press*. New York: Reinhold Publishing Corporation, 1966.

Gordon, Stephen F., and Jennifer D. Wyman. *Primer of Perception*. New York: Reinhold Publishing Corp., 1968.

Guild, Vera P. *Creative Use of Stitches*. Worcester, Mass.: Davis Publications, Inc., 1964.

Heller, Jules. *Printmaking Today*. New York: Holt, Rinehart and Winston, 1960.

Hill, Edward. *The Language of Drawing*. Englewood Cliffs, New Jersey: Prentice-Hall, 1968.

Johnson, Pauline. *Creating with Paper*. Seattle, Washington: University of Washington Press, 1958.

Kaupelis, Robert. *Learning to Draw*, New York: Watson Guptill Publications, 1966.

Krevitsky, Nik. *Batik: Art and Craft*. New York: Reinhold Publishing Corp., 1964.

————. *Stitchery: Art and Craft*. New York: Reinhold Publishing Corp., 1966.

La Liberte, Norman, and Maureen Jones. *Wooden Images*. New York: Reinhold Publishing Corp., 1967.

La Liberte, Norman, and Sterling McIlhany. *Banners and Hangings*. New York: Reinhold Publishing Corp., 1966.

La Liberte, Norman, and Alex Mogelon. *Drawing with Pencil*. New York: Reinhold Publishing Corp., 1969.

————. *Painting with Crayons*. New York: Reinhold Publishing Corp., 1967.

Lee, Ruth. *Exploring the World of Pottery*. Chicago, Illinois: Studio Children's Press, 1967.

Lynch, John. *How to Make Collages*. New York: The Viking Press, 1961.

————. *Metal Sculpture: New Forms, New Techniques*. New York: Studio Crowell, 1957.

————. *Mobile Design*. New York: Studio Crowell, 1955.

Meilach, Donna, and Ten Hoor. *Collage and Found Art*. New York: Reinhold Publishing Corp., 1964.

Mendelowitz, Daniel M. *Drawing*. New York: Holt, Rinehart and Winston, 1967.

Mills, John W. *The Techniques of Sculpture*. New York: Reinhold Publishing Corp., 1965.

Moseley, Spencer, Pauline Johnson, and Hazel Koenig. *Crafts Design*. Belmont, California: Wadsworth Publishing Co., 1962.

Mugnaini, Joseph, and Janice Lovoos. *Drawing: A Search for Form*. New York: Reinhold Publishing Corp., 1965.

Nelson, Glenn. *Ceramics*. New York: Holt, Rinehart and Winston, 1960.

Nicolaides, Kimon. *The Natural Way to Draw*. Boston: Houghton Mifflin Co., 1941.

Peterdi, Gabor. *Printmaking: Methods Old and New*. New York: Macmillan Company, 1959.

Petterson, Henry. *Creating Form in Clay*. New York: Reinhold Publishing Corp., 1968.

————, and Ray Gerring. *Exploring Paint*. New York: Reinhold Publishing Corp., 1964.

Randall, Reino, and E. C. Haines. *Design in Three Dimensions*. Worcester, Mass.: Davis Publications, Inc., 1965.

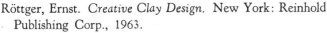

Röttger, Ernst. *Creative Clay Design*. New York: Reinhold Publishing Corp., 1963.

————. *Creative Wood Design*. New York: Reinhold Publishing Corp., 1960.

Seeler, Margarete. *The Art of Enamelling*. New York: Reinhold Publishing Corp., 1969.

Sneum, Gunnar. *Teaching Design and Form*. New York: Reinhold Publishing Corp., 1965.

Struppeck, Jules. *The Creation of Sculpture*. New York: Holt, Rinehart and Winston, 1952.

Supensky, Thomas G. *Ceramic Art in the School Program*. Worcester, Mass.: Davis Publications, Inc., 1968. The visual and technical information will definitely benefit the teacher of young adolescents.

Timmons, Virginia Gayheart. *Painting in the School Program*. Worcester, Mass.: Davis Publications, Inc., 1968.

Von Neumann, Robert. *The Design and Creation of Jewelry*. New York: Chilton, 1961.

Weaver, Peter. *Printmaking*. New York: Reinhold Book Corp., 1968.

Wigg, Philip R. *Introduction to Figure Drawing*. Dubuque, Iowa: Wm. C. Brown Company, 1967.

Willcox, Donald. *Wood Design*. Cincinnati, Ohio: Watson Guptill Publications, 1968.

Winter, Edward. *Enameling for Beginners*. New York: Watson Guptill Publications, 1962.

Woods, Gerald. *Introducing Woodcuts*. Cincinnati, Ohio: Watson Guptill Publications, 1969.

Designing an automobile license plate became the problem for seventh-grade youngsters, University School, Oshkosh, Wisconsin, which they resolved in plaster relief. The project began with a clay negative mold into which students pressed "found" objects or added ribbons or pellets of clay. (Process described on page 125.)

BOOKS ON ART APPRECIATION

Bauer, John I. H. *Nature in Abstraction*. New York: Macmillan Company, 1958.

Bethers, Ray. *Composition in Pictures*. New York: Pitman Publishing Corp., 1956.

———. *How Paintings Happen*. New York: Norton Publishers, 1951.

Canaday, John. *Keys to Art*. New York: Tudor Publishing Co., 1963.

Chase, A. E. *Looking at Art*. New York: Crowell, 1966.

Denny, Norman, and Josephine Filmer-Sankey. *The Bayeux Tapestry*. New York: Atheneum Publishers, Inc.

Downer, Marion. *Discovering Design*. New York: Lothrop, Lee and Shepard Co., 1947.

———. *The Story of Design*. New York: Lothrop, Lee and Shepard Co., 1963.

Faulkner, R., E. Ziegfeld, and G. Hill. *Art Today*, rev. ed. New York: Holt, Rinehart and Winston, Inc., 1963.

Feldman, Edmund Burke. *Art as Image and Idea*. Englewood Cliffs, New Jersey: Prentice-Hall, Inc., 1967. A scholarly yet highly readable text on the many aspects of art criticism. Should be in every art teacher's library.

Gettings, Fred. *The Meaning and Wonder of Art*. New York: Western Publishing Co., Inc., 1966.

Glubok, Shirley. *The Art of Africa*. New York: Harper and Row, 1965.

———. *The Art of Ancient Egypt*. New York: Antheneum Publishers Inc., 1963.

———. *The Art of Ancient Mexico*. New York: Harper and Row, 1966.

———. *The Art of Ancient Peru*. New York: Harper and Row, 1966.

———. *The Art of Ancient Rome*. New York: Harper and Row, 1965.

———. *The Art of the North American Indian*. New York: Harper and Row, 1964.

———. *The Arts of the Eskimo*. New York: Antheneum Publishers Inc., 1963.

Heyne, Carl J., and Florence W. Nicholas. *Art for Young America*, rev. ed. Peoria, Ill.: Chas. Bennett Co. Inc., 1968.

Jacobs, David. *Master Painters of the Renaissance*. New York: The Viking Press, 1968.

Kainz, C. Luise, and L. Olive Riley. *Understanding Art: People, Things and Ideas*. New York: Harry N. Abrams, Inc., 1966.

Kepes, Gyorgy. *Language of Vision*. Chicago: Paul Theobald, 1949.

———. *Sign, Image, Symbol*. New York: George Braziller, 1966.

Kuh, Katherine. *Art Has Many Faces*. New York: Harper and Bros., 1951.

Lowry, Bates. *The Visual Experience*. Englewood Cliffs, New Jersey: Prentice-Hall, Inc., 1965.

McIlhany, Sterling. *Art as Design: Design as Art*. New York: Reinhold Book Corp., 1969.

Parola, Rene. *Optical Art: Theory and Practice*. New York: Reinhold Book Corp., 1969.

Riley, L. Olive. *Masks and Magic*. New York: Studio Publications, 1955.

Schinneller, James A. *Art/Search and Self-Discovery*, 2d ed. Scranton, Pennsylvania: International Textbook Company, 1968. A newly-revised and handsome edition.

Opposite Page—Linoleum print. Middle school, Japan. Fish are a staple food in Japan; fresh-fish markets abound. This print reveals that the student is thoroughly familiar with varied fish forms, but beyond that, it shows a sensitive understanding of abstract design, of dark and light pattern, of space manipulation, of repetition of motifs to create unity.

PROFESSIONAL PUBLICATIONS

Bowie, Theodore. *Films on Art: A Critical Guide*. Bloomington, Indiana: Indiana University Audio-Visual Center, 1957.

Howell, Youldon C. (ed.). *8th Yearbook of the National Art Education Association*. Kutztown, Pennsylvania: National Art Education Association, 1957.

Humphys, Alfred W. *Films on Art*. Washington, D.C.: National Art Education Association, 1965.

Lally, Ann M. (ed.). *Art Education in the Secondary School*. Washington, D.C.: National Art Education Association, 1964.

Michael, John A. (ed.). *Art Education in the Junior High School*. Washington, D.C.: National Art Education Association, 1964. Excellent treatment of adolescent characteristics, art laboratory facilities, and materials and visual aids.

The Museum and the Art Teacher. Research report by U.S. Office of Health, Education and Welfare, 1966. Project director: Jerome J. Hausman.

Planning Facilities for Art Instruction. Washington, D.C.: National Art Education Association.

Reproductions and Paperback Books on Art. Washington, D.C.: National Art Education Association, 1967.

Slides and Filmstrips on Art. Washington, D.C.: National Art Education Association, 1966.

Space and Facilities for Art Instruction. Publication #9, Cat. #FS5.221:21025, Washington, D.C.: U.S. Department of Health, Education and Welfare, 1963. Superintendent of Documents, Washington, D.C. 20402.

A magazine photograph became the inspiration for this charcoal drawing by a junior high school student from Clarke County Junior High School, Athens, Georgia.

CURRICULUM GUIDES

Art Education and the Adolescent. Bulletin D-Four. Springfield, Ill.: Office of Superintendent of Public Instruction, Illinois Curriculum Program, 1962.

Instruction and Curriculum in Glendale. California Junior High School, 1962.

Secondary Art Guide. Olympia, Washington: State Superintendent of Public Instruction, 1965.

Ways to Art. Curriculum Division Publication #SC 424, *Art: Seventh Grade,* rev. 1952. Los Angeles, Calif.: Los Angeles City School Districts, 1952.

FILMS

Number indicates length of film in minutes. C indicates color; B/W, black and white. Last letters indicate distributor. Complete addresses for film and filmstrip distributors are listed following filmstrip listing.

The American Vision. 36/C. EBF.
Ancient Art of Peru. 15/C. FI.
Ancient Egypt. 11/C. COR.
Ancient Greece. 11/C. COR.
Ancient Orient: The Far East. 13½/C. COR.
Ancient Rome. 11/C. COR.
Art and Architecture. 3 films, 30/C each. EBF.
Art and Life in Italy. 11/C. COR.
Art and Motion. 17/C. EBF.
Art and You. 11/C. FA.
Art in the Western World. 30/C. COR.
Art—What is it? Why is it? 30/C. EBF.

A middle school youngster from England achieved a distinctively melancholy mood in this charcoal drawing of a classmate that no photograph could capture as well. Courtesy of LONDON SUNDAY MIRROR.

FILMSTRIPS AND LOOPS

Art Media, Art Elements. Film loops. EAL.

The Art of Seeing; 6 filmstrips with records. A Warren Schloat Production. PREN.

Art by Talented Teen-agers; 1961–66, 1967, 1968, 1969. SCHOL.

Collected Works of Teen-age Art by Category; 1961–66. SCHOL.

Composition in Nature; 6 color filmstrips, average 32 frames per strip. BF.

European Art; 12 filmstrips, 25 frames per strip. BF.

Exploring Art Techniques; 4 color filmstrips, average 50 frames per strip. BF.

Introduction to Graphic Design; 2 color filmstrips, average 50 frames per strip. BF.

Japanese Prints; color with narration on 33⅓ RPM Record. IFC.

Learning to Look; 6 color filmstrips, average 33 frames per strip. BF.

Listening, Looking, and Feeling; 4 filmstrips, 26–30 frames per strip. BF.

Looking for Composition; 3 color filmstrips, average of 30 frames per strip. BF.

Masters of the Japanese Print; filmstrip set, 4 color filmstrips, 30 frames each. BF.

Masterworks of Mexican Art; sound filmstrip set, 6 color filmstrips, 42–62 frames. BF.

Meet the Artist; 5 color filmstrips on Van Gogh, Rembrandt, Renoir, Picasso, and Wyeth with records. MIL.

Mosaics for All; 3 color filmstrips, average 37 frames per strip. BF.

Seeing Trees and Clouds; 4 color filmstrips with average of 40 frames per strip. BF.

ADDRESSES OF FILM AND FILMSTRIP COMPANIES

AF	Associated Films, 247 Madison Avenue, New York, New York.
AHC	American Handicrafts Company, 83 West Van Buren Street, Chicago, Illinois.
BF	Bailey Films, 6509 De Longpre Avenue, Hollywood, California.
BRAN	Brandon Films Incorporated, 200 West 57th Street, New York, New York.
CON	Contemporary Films Incorporated, 267 West 25th Street, New York, New York.
COR	Coronet Films, 65 East South Water Street, Chicago, Illinois.
EAL	Ealing Film Loops, 2225 Massachusetts Avenue, Cambridge, Massachusetts.
EBF	Encyclopedia Brittanica Films, 1150 Wilmette Avenue, Wilmette, Illinois.
FA	Film Associates of California, 11014 Santa Monica Boulevard, Los Angeles, California
FI	Film Images Incorporated, 1860 Broadway, New York, New York.

FPS	Film Production Service, Virginia Department of Education, Richmond, Virginia.
IFC	Imperial Film Company, Inc., Lakeland, Florida.
IFB	International Film Bureau Incorporated, 332 South Michigan Avenue, Chicago, Illinois.
LAR	Louis de Rochemont Associates, Film Library, 13 East 37th Street, New York, New York.
MIL	Miller Brody Productions Incorporated, 342 Madison Avenue, New York, New York.
MMA	Museum of Modern Art, 11 West 53rd Street, New York, New York.
NFBC	National Film Board of Canada, 680 Fifth Avenue, New York, New York.
SF	Santa Fe Film Bureau, 80 Jackson Boulevard, Chicago, Illinois.
SCHOL	Scholastic Filmstrips, 906 Sylvan Avenue, Englewood Cliffs, New Jersey.
UNESCO	Unesco Publications Center, 317 East 34th St., New York, New York.

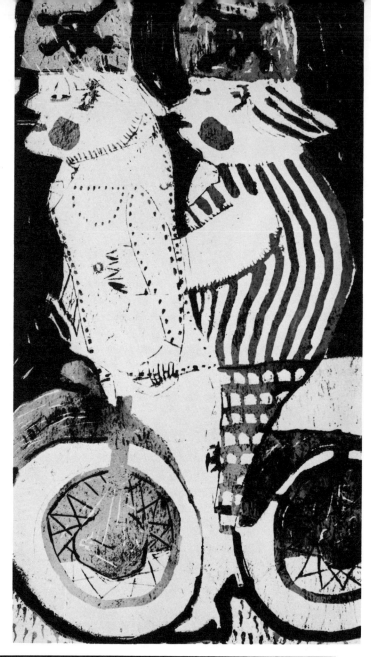

Left—Experimental photography. Clarke County Junior High School, Athens, Georgia. Right—Lino reduction print. Middle school, England. Courtesy of LONDON SUNDAY MIRROR.

C

ART SUPPLIES AND SOURCES

One of the first responsibilities beginning teachers face upon appointment to a position as art instructor in a school is the preparation and submission of an art supply list or budget for their classes. Often the school administration requires this information before the term begins. This is especially true where new junior high art programs are being offered for the first time either in new buildings or remodeled classrooms.

It is important therefore that the teacher's college preparation in art include a realistic survey of materials, tools and equipment commonly in use in the school art programs together with the sources of supply. A variety of art media should be explored and exploited by the interning teachers in their methods and procedures courses. Art supply firms will provide teachers with their current materials catalogs if the request is made on school stationery.

An excellently detailed listing of basic art supplies, tools and equipment for the young adolescents' program is provided in the 1964 NAEA publication *Art Education in the Junior High School*. Another highly recommended secondary school art supply listing is found in the 1962 Illinois Bulletin D-Four, *Art Education and the Adolescent* available at cost from the Office of the Superintendent of Public Instruction, Springfield, Ill.

The following items, supplies and tools have been found especially useful by the authors in the implementation of the junior or middle school art program. They are listed here with possible project utilization.

ITEM	USE	SOURCE
Aggregate (Perlite, Zonolite, vermiculite, Terra-lite)	Mix with plaster of Paris molds or reliefs for textural effects and ease in carving	Lumber dealer
Applicator sticks	For constructions, stabiles, mobiles, collages	Drug store
Balsa wood	In blocks or sheets for carving or construction	Arts and crafts supply firms
Baren hand press	Device for taking a print	Dick Blick Co.
Beaverboard (Upson board) Available in sheets 4′ x 8′ and 1/4 or 3/8 inch thick	For use as sketching or drawing boards, or as protection for desk or table tops. Secure edges by overlapping with 3/4 inch masking tape. Coat with latex paint if desired	Lumber dealer

ITEM	USE	SOURCE
Brayers	Rubber rollers in neoprene or soft gum for inking in printmaking	Dick Blick Co.; Sax Arts and Crafts
Brilliants (Alphacolor)	Semi-moist watercolor cakes. Opaque	Weber Costello Co.
Burlap (assorted colors)	For stitchery projects, appliqué, or for use in displays	Department and mail order stores
Carving wax	Available in blocks and assorted colors for sculpture projects	Dick Blick Co.
Cellotex, ½ inch thick	As a working surface for reed, stick, or straw stabiles	Lumber dealer
Cement (Testor Formula AA, fast-drying airplane glue)	As an adhesive for straw, stick, reed or toothpick constructions	Arts and crafts supply firms
Craypas	Oil pastel medium for picture making, for murals and designing; oil pastels are now available from several arts and crafts firms	Art supply firms
Crea-stone	Cast stone mix for carving projects	Dick Blick Co.
Dextrin	Adhesive in powder form; add 5 to 10 percent to earth clay to achieve hardening without firing	Drug store
Duco cement	For effective gluing of parts in construction projects	Arts and crafts supply firms
Easycurve board	For constructions where a strong yet pliable cardboard is needed	Lumber dealer
Featherstone	Grained volcanic ash for carving; light weight, porous; gloves are recommended during carving process	Dick Blick Co.
Firebrick	A lightweight, porous refractory brick for carving projects	Lumber dealer or ceramics supply
Foamglass	Carving medium, black, fine-grain cellular glass; a well-ventilated working area is necessary.	Pittsburgh Plate Glass or Dick Blick Co.

ITEM	USE	SOURCE
Formaldehyde	A few drops in liquid media (tempera, finger-paint) will prevent souring. *Phenol* can be substituted for similar results	Drug store
Gesso	Plaster of Paris solution conditioned with glue; apply to papier-mâché sculpture for a smooth painting surface	Arts and crafts supply firms
Glycerin	Mix with honey and powder tempera to make a monoprint medium	Drug store
Hyplar medium	For adhering tissue in collages or papier-mâché constructions	M. Grumbacher, Inc.
Ink platen	Laminated plastic surface for inking in print-making projects: 10″ by 12″ or 12″ by 15″ sizes	Dick Blick Co.
Laundry starch	For applying colored tissue in collage process	Food market
Masonite	For working surfaces in clay projects (use tempered 12″ by 12″ pieces varnished or lacquered), for sketching boards, for surface support in rinse-off process of tempera batiks, for table or desk tops	Lumber dealer
Mat knife	For cutting mats or mounts	Arts and crafts supply firms
Niji	Oil pastels for picture making, designing	Arts and crafts supply firms
Paraffin	For coating cardboard boxes prior to pouring plaster of Paris mold; in sheets for printmaking surfaces	Food market
Paris craft	Plaster-impregnated gauze available in varied widths for 3-D constructions over armatures	Arts and crafts supply firms
Pastoil	Oil pastels for painting and picture making	Permanent Pigments, Inc.

ITEM	USE	SOURCE
Pentel	Water-soluble, fast drying oil paints; also oil pastels of same brand	Pentel of America, Ltd.
Plaster of Paris	Sift into water for making sculpture molds, reliefs, spoon jewelry, applied sculpture, or printmaking surfaces	Lumber dealer
Polytemps	Polymer tempera in semi-moist cakes; opaque, matte finish; snap-on lids	Arts and crafts supply firms
Press (Universal)	For heavy-duty printmaking; table model; two interchangeable beds, one flat, one for type-high block; cushion roller; many other models available from same source	Dick Blick Co.
PVA (Poly Vinyl Acetate)	Adhesive with many uses such as adhering plastic tile or tessera to glass	Arts and crafts supply firms
Railroad board	A glossy surface cardboard available in assorted colors; recommended for background paper in multi-crayon engravings	Arts and crafts supply firms
Rub 'n' Buff	Metallic finishes and varied patinas for sculpture and construction projects	Arts and crafts supply firms
Sculpmetal	Metal in paste form which can be applied as patina over wire, plaster of Paris, or papier-mâché sculptures; burnish with steel wool	Arts and crafts supply firms

ITEM	USE	SOURCE
Sculpstone	Boulder size blocks of carving material; available in pure white, translucent or cream color; slight grain and texture	Dick Blick Co.
Shreddimix	A papier-mâché mix which can be molded and pressed into forms	Arts and crafts supply firms
Sloyd knife	The short-bladed version is recommended for carving projects, for crayon and multi-crayon engraving techniques	Brodhead-Garrett Co.
Tempera blocks (Reeves)	Tempera in solid form in six intermixable colors; *Tidy Tubs* of semi-solid watercolor cakes available from same source	Dick Blick Co.
Tissue paper	Available in many colors for use in tissue collage, mixed-media collage, surface decoration on papier-mâché sculptures	Arts and crafts supply firms
Transfer paper	White dressmaker's carbon for use in transferring preliminary sketches to dark surfaces as in crayon engraving process	Orco Products, Inc. 275 Leo Street Dayton, Ohio
White liquid glues	Elmer's, Wilhold, Sobo for general use in various projects	Arts and crafts supply firms
X-ray plates (discards)	For acetate engravings; must be cleaned first by rinsing in laundry bleach	Hospitals and clinics

Major art supply companies are listed below for the teacher's reference. More complete listings are published regularly in *School Arts, Arts and Activities,* and *American Artist* magazines.

Aiko's (Oriental Supplies), 714 North Wabash, Chicago, Ill. 60611.

Allcraft Tool and Supply Co., Inc., 215 Park Ave., Hicksville, N.Y. 11801.

American Art Clay Co., 4717 West 16th St., Indianapolis, Ind. 46222.

American Crayon Company, 1706 Hayes Ave., Sandusky, Ohio 44870.

Austen Display, Inc., 133 West 19th St., New York, N.Y. 10011.

Binney and Smith, Inc., 380 Madison Ave., New York, N.Y. 10017.

Brodhead-Garret Co., 4560 East 71st St., Cleveland, Ohio 44105.

The Craftool Company, Industrial Road, Woodridge, N.J. 07075.

Crystal Tissue Co., South Verity Parkway, Middletown, Ohio 45042.

Delta Brush Mfg. Corp., 120 S. Columbus Ave., Mt. Vernon, New York 10553.

Dick Blick Co., P.O. Box 1267, Galesburg, Ill. 61401.

Higgins Ink Co., Inc., 271 Ninth Street, Brooklyn, N.Y. 11215.

Hunt Mfg. Co., 1405 Locust St., Philadelphia, Pa. 19102.

M. Grumbacher, Inc., 472 West 34th St., New York, N.Y. 10001.

Milton Bradley Company, 74 Park St., Springfield, Mass. 01101.

Pentel of America, Ltd., 333 N. Michigan Ave., Chicago, Ill. 60601.

Permanent Pigments, Inc., 2700 Highland Ave., Cincinnati, Ohio 45212.

Sanford Ink Company, Bellwood, Illinois 60104.

Sax Arts and Crafts, 207 N. Milwaukee Ave., Milwaukee, Wis. 53202.

Stafford Reeves Incorporated, 626 Greenwich St., New York, N.Y. 10014.

Talens and Son, Inc., Iorio Court, Union, N.J. 07083.

Triarco Arts and Crafts, Box 106, Northfield, Ill. 60093.

Weber Costello Company, 1900 N. Narragansett Ave., Chicago, Ill. 60639.

Winsor and Newton, 555 Winsor Drive, Secaucus, N.J. 17194.

Yasutomo and Co. (Oriental Supplies), 24 California St., San Francisco, Cal. 94111.

Opposite Page—Steps in a mixed-media collage project by students in the author's secondary art methods class, University of Georgia. Both compositions began with a preliminary drawing. Left—A cityscape. Right—The steering compartment of a station wagon.

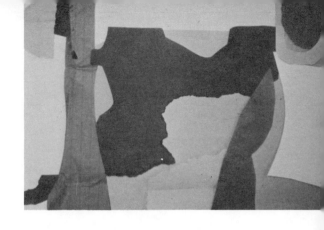

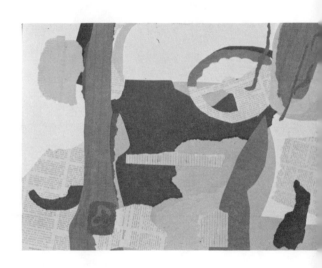

appendix

D

GLOSSARY

Abstract art—an interpretation that expresses the essence of a figure, object, or place in lines, geometric forms, or planes with little regard for its natural appearance.

Acetone—a solvent for plastics.

Aesthetic—appreciative of, or responsive to, the beautiful in art or nature.

Alcohol—a solvent for shellac (methanol or shellacol).

Armature—framework used to support modeling substances such as clay, papier-mâché, or plaster (usually made of wood, metal, or wire mesh).

Asymmetric—a balance in art composition based on an informal or occult relationship.

Balsa—a strong, light wood for carving, construction, model building, or for collages (available in sheets, strips, or blocks).

Baren—a Japanese product used as a pressure device in rubbing the paper when taking a woodblock print.

Bas-relief—low relief sculpture (the opposite of incised relief).

Bat—a flat, level plaster slab used to absorb moisture from wet clay. (A bat can be easily cast by pouring prepared plaster of Paris into a vaseline-coated rubberized dishpan.)

Batik—a method of creating colored designs on fabric by coating with wax those areas not to be dyed (term also used to describe resist techniques).

Biomorphic—related to life or living organisms.

Bisque or biscuit—unglazed pottery after first firing.

Blot drawing—the practice of evolving a composition from the forms suggested by allowing a few blots of ink or color to fall at random on a sheet of paper.

Opposite Page—Cut-out paper design from middle school, Germany. Courtesy of Pelikan Company, Hannover, West Germany. The "Trojan Horse" is a familiar theme in art for youngsters in many countries. Complex cut-out paper designs as this are common in Germany, Poland, and Czechoslovakia.

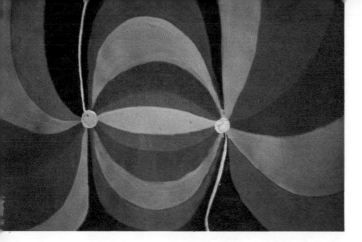

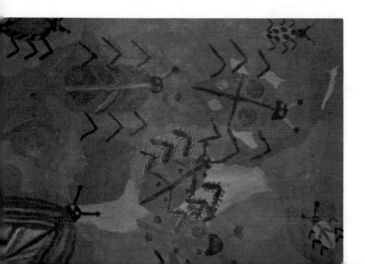

Brayer—rubber roller used in inking printing blocks (gelatin brayers are also available).

Bronze—metal used for casting sculpture. A substance which can also be hammered into shapes.

Burin or graver—the principal tool used in engraving on wood or metal to plough the lines out of the surface of the plate or block.

Burnish—to make smooth or shiny by a rubbing or polishing action.

Burr—a rough ridge in metal, clay, or other substances created by a gouging tool passing through the surface area.

Charcoal—black marker made from twigs of willow or vine which have been charred. Charcoal is sometimes used for drawings on paper, but its principal use is for making the preliminary drawings on walls or canvases as the first stage in a painting.

Chiaroscuro (Italian)—as generally used, the balance of light and shadow in a picture and the skill shown by the painter in the management of shadows.

Chipboard—heavy cardboard, usually gray, for use in painting, collage, construction, and cardboard prints.

Chroma—another designation for color or hue.

Collage—composition made by assembling, pasting, and gluing materials to a surface (can be combined with drawing, painting, and glazing).

174

Students find color has the magic to suggest moods, feelings, sounds, and imaginative worlds. Top—A bold complementary color abstraction. English middle school. Middle—The deep sea interpreted in cool hues. West Germany. Bottom—Warm colors predominate in this design. West Germany.

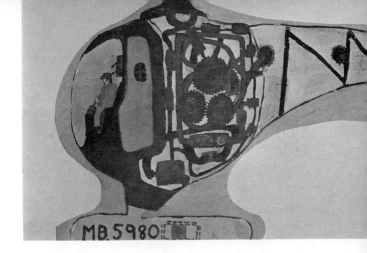

Colors: *Primary*—red, yellow, blue; three basic hues which cannot be produced by a mixture of pigments.

Secondary—orange, green, purple; colors achieved by mixing primaries.

Tertiary—colors derived by mixing secondaries; sometimes called intermediate hues.

Analogous—colors, closely related, neighbors on the color wheel—yellow, yellow-orange and red, for example.

Complementary—colors opposite each other on the color wheel—sharply contrasting hues.

Triad—color equidistant from each other on the color wheel.

Warm—colors usually associated with fire, sun, and earth—red, orange, brown.

Cool—colors usually associated with water, sky, spring, and foliage—green, blue, turquoise.

Composition—the art of combining the elements of a picture or other work of art into a satisfactory visual whole; in art, the whole is much more than the sum of the parts.

Cones—miniature clay pyramids which melt at a given temperature and measure the heat during kiln firing.

Contour—a line drawing delineating the external characteristics or boundaries of a shape or form.

The adolescent is concerned with life around him. Teachers can capitalize on this growing interest by suggesting social themes as subjects for art. Top—Helicopter by youngster from England. Courtesy of London Sunday Mirror. *Middle—New Delhi, India. International exhibit. Bottom—Bicycle race. Santarcangelo, Italy.*

175

Coping saw—a small hand saw used to cut circular and irregular shapes in plywood, Upson board, masonite, etc.

Design—an ordered, aesthetic arrangement of one or more of the components of art: line, value, shape, form, color, or texture.

Dowel—a thin pole of wood available in graded dimensions.

Empathy—the projection of one's personality into the object of contemplation, a feeling-into.

Emphasis—a principle in design or composition which connotes importance or significance. It often implies both dominance and subordination.

Encaustic—a painting technique in which colors are mixed with wax and applied to a surface.

Engobe—liquid clay or slip applied as color for surface decoration in ceramics; should be applied while clay is damp.

Engraving—the process of incising or scratching into metal or other prepared surfaces with a sharp tool.

Expression—in art, a subjective interpretation of sensations, emotions, or ideas, rather than of actual appearances.

Expressionism—a style of exaggeration and distortion of line and color; a deliberate abandonment of naturalism in favor of a style of greater emotional impact.

Fixatif—a commercial preparation in liquid or spray form used to protect easily-smudged surfaces.

Flux—a material applied to a point to be soldered to prevent oxides from forming when the metal is heated.

Focal point—a point or spot of interest in a composition where the observer's eye comes to rest.

Foot—in ceramics the foot of a pot or container.

Form—usually a sculptural or three-dimensional shape defined by its characteristic contour.

"Found" object—any kind of object, such as a shell found on a walk. "Found" objects can be used as components in a work of art.

Fresco—a painting on freshly applied plaster (true fresco).

Frottage—a design created by rubbing an oil or wax crayon on thin paper placed over objects with raised surface qualities, such as reliefs, mosaics, collages, or natural forms such as feathers, leaves or wood grains.

Gelatin—transparent theatrical color modulator available in multiple colors.

Genre—compositions which emphasize everyday events.

Gesso—the name given to the ground used in tempera painting and in certain types of oil painting. It is a dense and brilliantly white ground with a high degree of absorbancy.

Glaze—a transparent or opaque surface finish applied to ceramic or metalware.

Glazing—the process of applying a transparent layer of oil paint over a solid one so that the color of the first is modified.

Gouache—an opaque watercolor paint (known to many people as poster paint).

Greenware—unfired ceramic ware; leather hard stage, when clay is firm but not quite fully dry.

Grog—fired clay ground to a powder; provides porosity and texture in clay pieces to be fired.

Ground—the surface on which painting is made.

Mixed-media collage by eighth-grade student, Oshkosh, Wisconsin. The interests of the young adolescent—sports, bicycling, TV, singing combos, movies, school events—all can add to his repertoire of subject matter for art. Note here how the rider fills the space, the feeling of motion achieved by the flowing scarf, the sharp, strong values for contrast.

Hatching—a system for building up tones or shadows by using a series of lines at various angles (cross-hatching).

Horizon line—an imaginary line, usually at the eye level of the observer, where the sky seems to meet the earth.

Hue—color or chroma.

Impasto—a particularly thick or heavy application of paint.

Impressionism—the derisive name given to the most important artistic phenomenon of the 19th century and the first of the Modern Movements. The name was derived from a picture by Monet, Impression, Sunrise (1872).

Intaglio—an engraved design, the opposite of relief.

Intensity—in reference to color, its brightness or dullness.

Kiln—(pronounced "kill") an oven or furnace for drying, firing, or glazing ceramic ware or metal enamelled ware.

Kiln wash—a protective coating that prevents excessive glaze from sticking to kiln shelves.

Line—a mark made by a moving point.

Linear composition—a composition which depends for its effect on the pattern made by the outlines of the forms represented, rather than on the masses of tone and color.

Lithography—a process of printing from a stone or prepared metal plate involving the use of a grease crayon and ink.

Local color—the positive or natural color of an object, for example, leaf-green, lemon-yellow, sky-blue.

Masonite—a pressed board made from steam-exploded wood fibers; can be used for drawing boards, clay boards, table tops, inking surfaces, and construction projects.

Mass—a large form or substantial area of color or value.

Mat board—a heavy poster board used for mounting pictures, specimens, and other displays.

Matte (or mat)—a term describing a dull, flat, nonglossy surface or sheen.

Medium—any material used for art expression, such as clay, paint, wood, or metal.

Mobile—a kind of sculpture in which the parts move; usually of metal.

Sometimes adolescents are intrigued by problems in perspective. Here a student in a middle school, Tokyo, Japan, interprets an end of a school hallway in a rather free approach which nevertheless exhibits a knowledge of converging lines.

Modelling—the three-dimensional representation of forms by means of some plastic material, usually clay. The opposite of carving.

Monochromatic—referring to one-color interpretation.

Monoprint—a type of surface printing in which the design is created on a hard surface such as glass with oil, ink, or fingerpaint. The composition is then transferred to the paper by contact.

Montage—the sticking of one layer over another, especially as in photomontage when photographs of objects are applied to a photograph of an unusual or incongruous background.

Mosaic—a design or composition formed by the planned juxtaposition of clay, plastic or glass tesserae cemented in grout or mortar.

Motif—center or dominant theme or feature.

Mural—a wall painting, usually performing an architectonic function.

Nonobjective art—expressions of pure form design which bear no resemblance to natural objects.

Papier-mâché—a substance made of paper pulp conditioned with sizing or paste.

Pastel—another name for colored chalk or description for the tint of a color.

Patina—the greenish incrustation on the surface of old bronze. It is esteemed for it own sake, and the word has had its meaning extended to cover all forms of mellowing with age.

Peeling—separation of slip from surface of pot during firing.

Perspective—a system for the representation of three-dimensional objects in spatial recession on a two-dimensional surface.

Picture plane—the extreme front edge of the imaginary space in a picture.

Plaster of Paris—a white powder (calcium sulfate) which, when mixed with water, forms a quick-setting casting or construction material; also used for clay bats.

Plasticity—the quality of appearing three-dimensional.

The line drawing still remains the basic concern for young artists. Here a vase of flowers by a Japanese youngster shows the skill the young adolescent can develop to make an aesthetic statement about his everyday environment.

179

Positive-negative—positive areas in a composition are definite forms and shapes; negative areas are the unoccupied or empty spaces.

Priming—the first coat on which all subsequent paint layers are applied. For oil-painting on canvas, the sized canvas is usually primed with white lead or gesso.

Proportion—the relation of one part to a whole or to other parts.

Pyrometer—a device for measuring the temperature in kiln firing.

Radiation—divergent lines, forms, or colors emanating from a central point of interest.

Raffia—a palm fiber available in a wide range of colors for use in weaving and constructions.

Recession—the name given to the phenomenon of objects in a picture appearing to recede into the depth of the imaginary picture space.

Relief—sculpture which is not free-standing, and in aspect approximates the condition of painting. See bas or incised relief.

Repoussé—metal work in which the design is hammered into a relief form from the reverse side.

Rhythm—an ordered movement created by the repetition of pictorial elements.

Rubber cement—a clean, quick-drying, latex type of cement or glue.

Scoring—to mark with grooves using an edged tool—as in paper sculpture or clay welding.

Scumble—a painting term referring to the softening of a color by the application of another opaque color over it.

Slip—clay mixed with water to consistency of cream. Used like glue to fasten pieces or surfaces of clay together. Also can be used in clay decoration and incised reliefs.

Stabile—a design in space made of wire, string, or other affinitive materials, mounted on a base.

Stained glass—consists of designs or figures made from pieces of colored glass held together by strips of lead, which themselves form the outlines of a design partly independent of the colored patches.

Stump—a cigar-shaped roll of paper, sharply pointed at each end, which is used to rub charcoal or chalk drawings so as to obtain very delicate transitions of tone.

Symbol—in art, the representation of an object, idea, or quality through an intermediate figure, sign or geometric character.

Tactile—referring to the sense of touch.

Tempera—an opaque, water-soluble paint in which the pigment is mixed with an albuminous substance.

Terra cotta—a red earth-colored clay body with a high grog content.

Tessera—a small, geometric segment of glass, marble, plastic, stone, or similar material used in mosaic work.

Texture—the actual and/or visual feel of a surface; the representation of the tactile character of a given material.

Tint—a graduation of a color achieved by mixing it with white pigment or diluting it with a solvent.

Value—an attribute of color, its lightness or darkness; for example, the values of red might range from pink to maroon.

Vanishing point—in perspective drawings, a point or points to which all lines recede.

Vermiculite—a form of mica or insulation material, generally used as an aggregate in plaster of Paris carving blocks or relief molds.

Vitrification—the process of becoming glass-like, as in a glaze, or nonporous, as in ceramics.

Volume—in art, usually a form or mass with three-dimensional or solid implications.

Wedging—a method of preparing clay by kneading it to expel air pockets.

Welding—in clay modeling, the process of adhering two pieces of clay with slip and/or scoring procedures.

We close reluctantly with the subtly and sensitively painted water color by a seventh-grade youngster from Japan. Evidence of the young teenager's expressive potential, his ability to master a technique and to stay with a project in depth, as this painting and other illustrations in the book reveal, should be of deep concern to those who guide today's youth.

We hope it will reinforce every middle school or junior high school art teacher's commitment to continually encourage in-depth art experiences for his students. The unique creative energies and capabilities of the young adolescent have in too many instances gone untapped and unrecognized. It is time indeed for a reevaluation of art teaching purposes and practices.

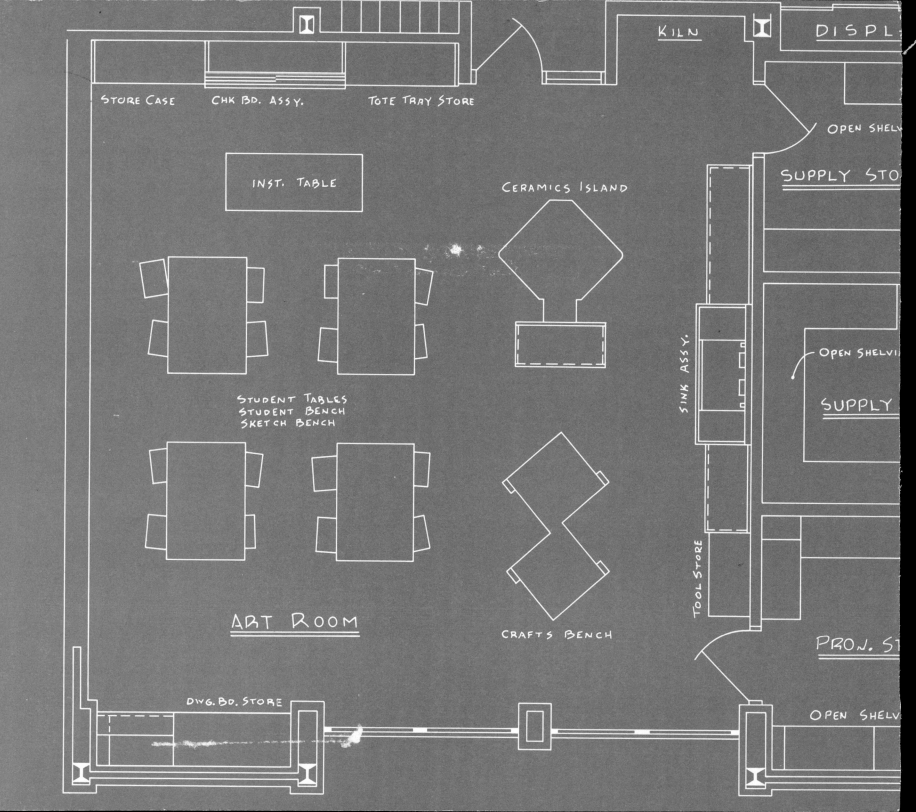

KILN

DISPL

STORE CASE   CHK BD. ASSY.   TOTE TRAY STORE

OPEN SHELV

SUPPLY STO

INST. TABLE

CERAMICS ISLAND

OPEN SHELVI

SUPPLY

STUDENT TABLES
STUDENT BENCH
SKETCH BENCH

SINK ASSY.

TOOL STORE

ART ROOM

CRAFTS BENCH

PROJ. ST

DWG. BD. STORE

OPEN SHELV

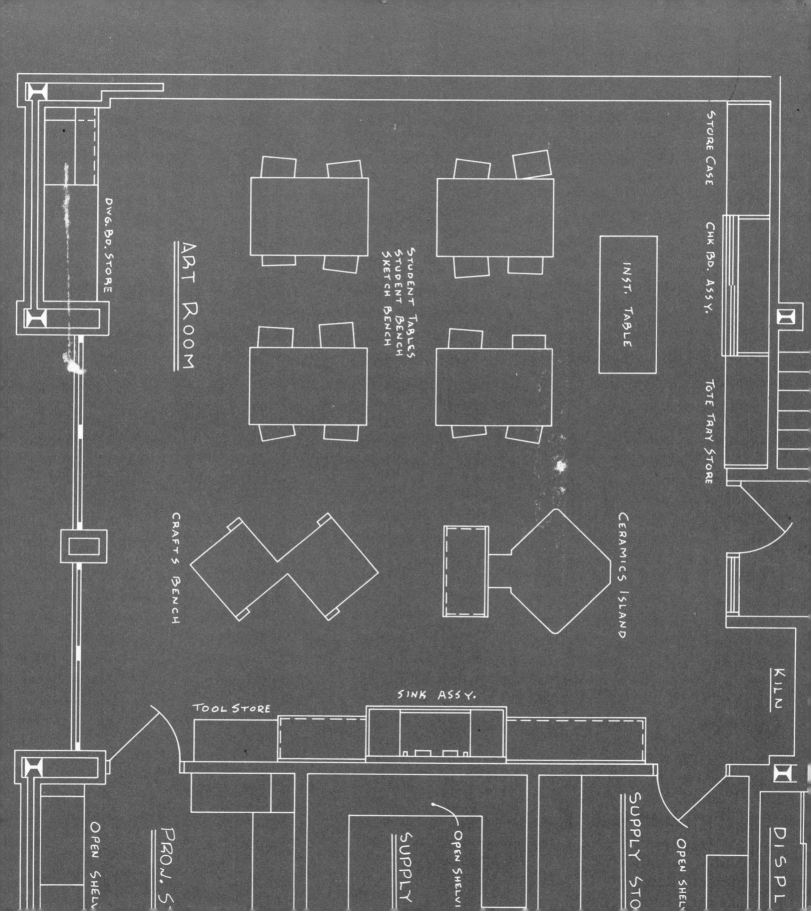